Dedication:

For all the little adventurers and artists who dare to explore the world of imagination and color. May this book transport you to the depths of the jungle, where creativity flourishes and the magic of nature is found on every page. May each stroke of color be a reminder of how special you are and of the infinite power that resides within each of you. May these pages teeming with life be a constant reminder that with courage and imagination, there are no limits to what you can achieve. May "Colorful Jungle" be the beginning of many colorful adventures and dreams come true. With love and admiration, Jomar Cardozo.

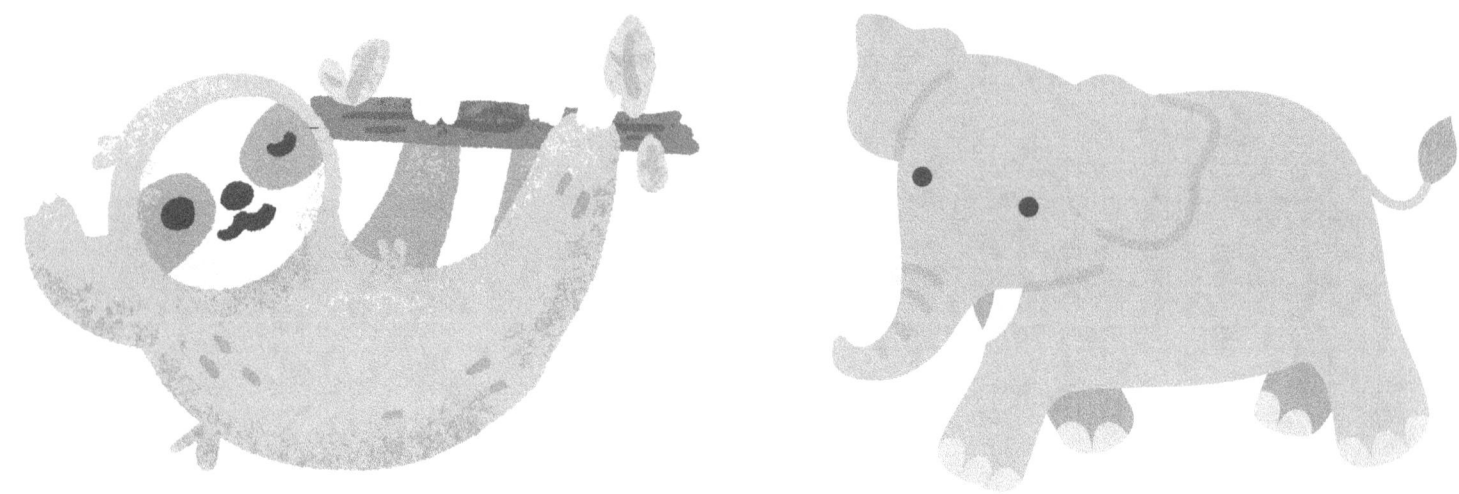

This book belong:

_____

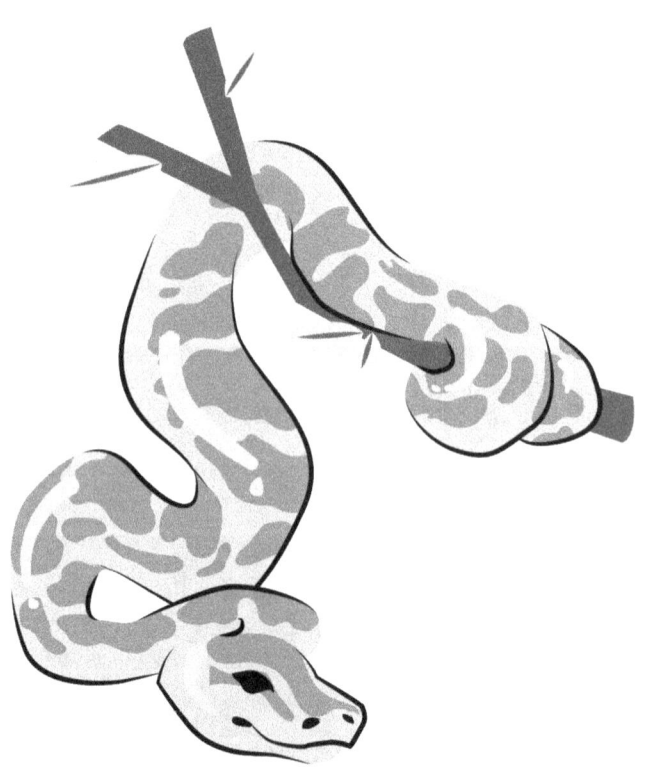

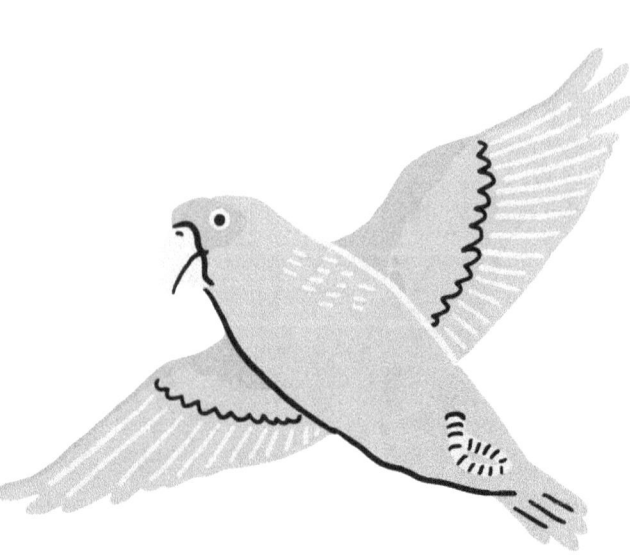

All Rights reserved©

Test color page

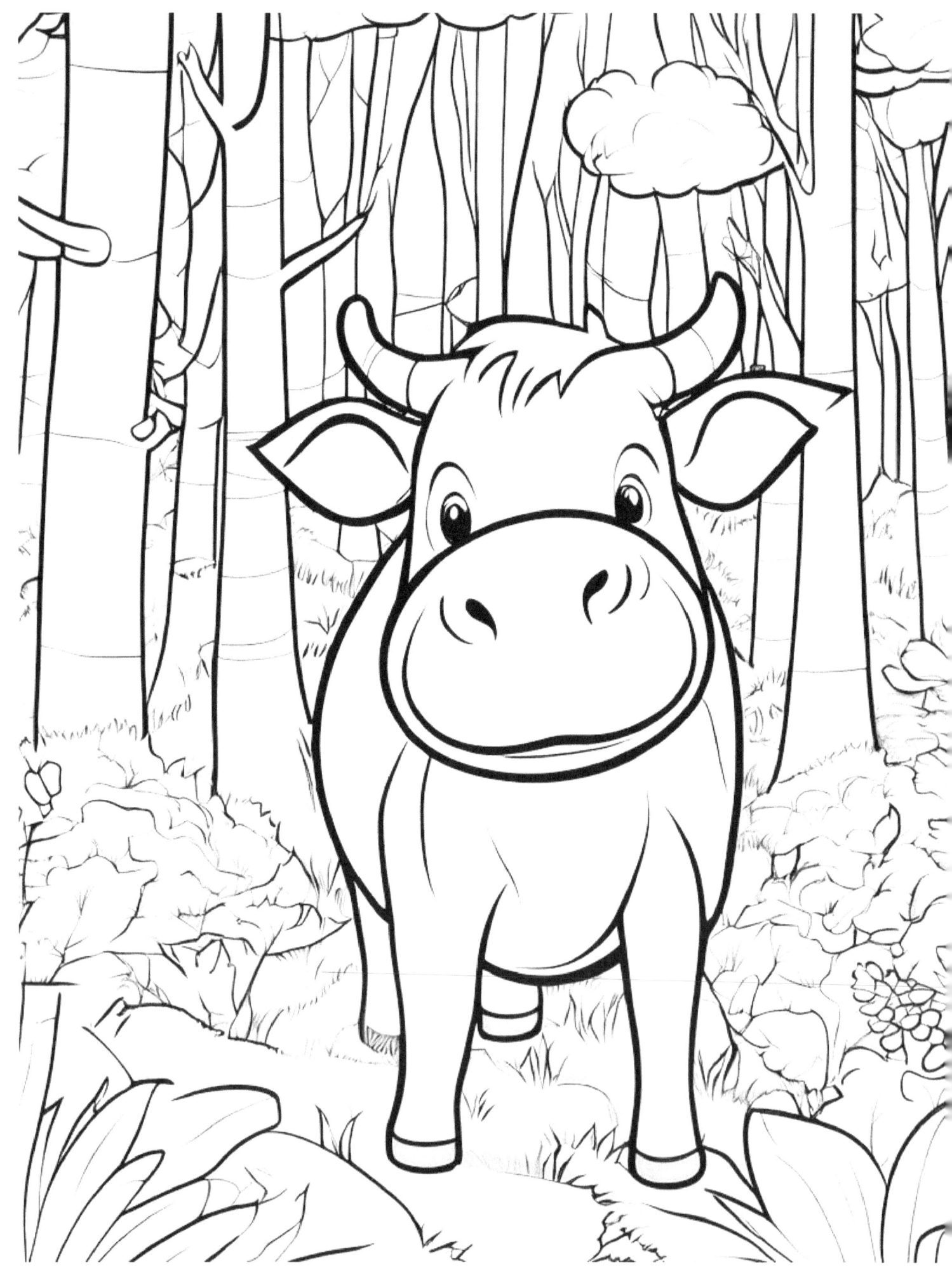

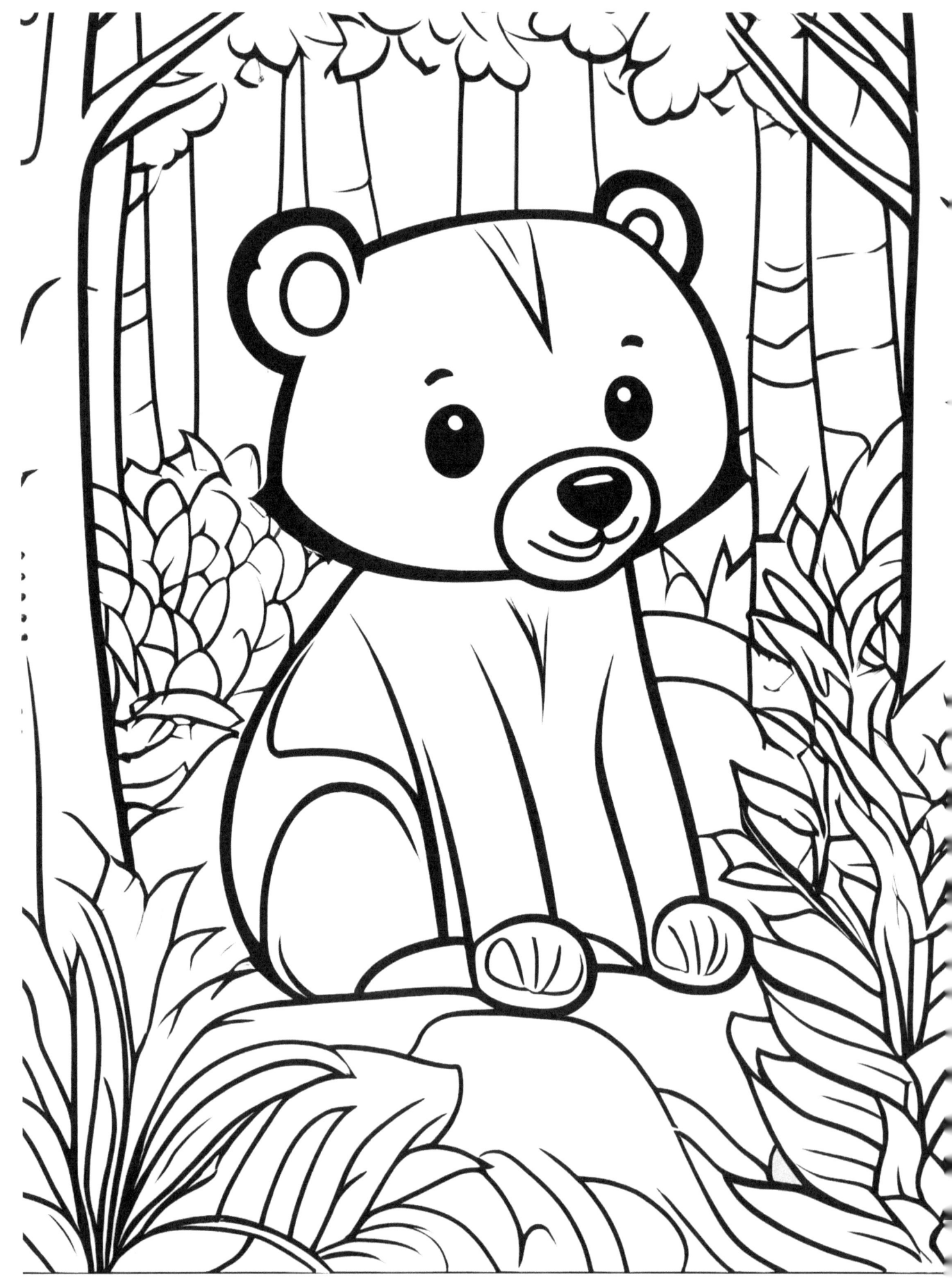

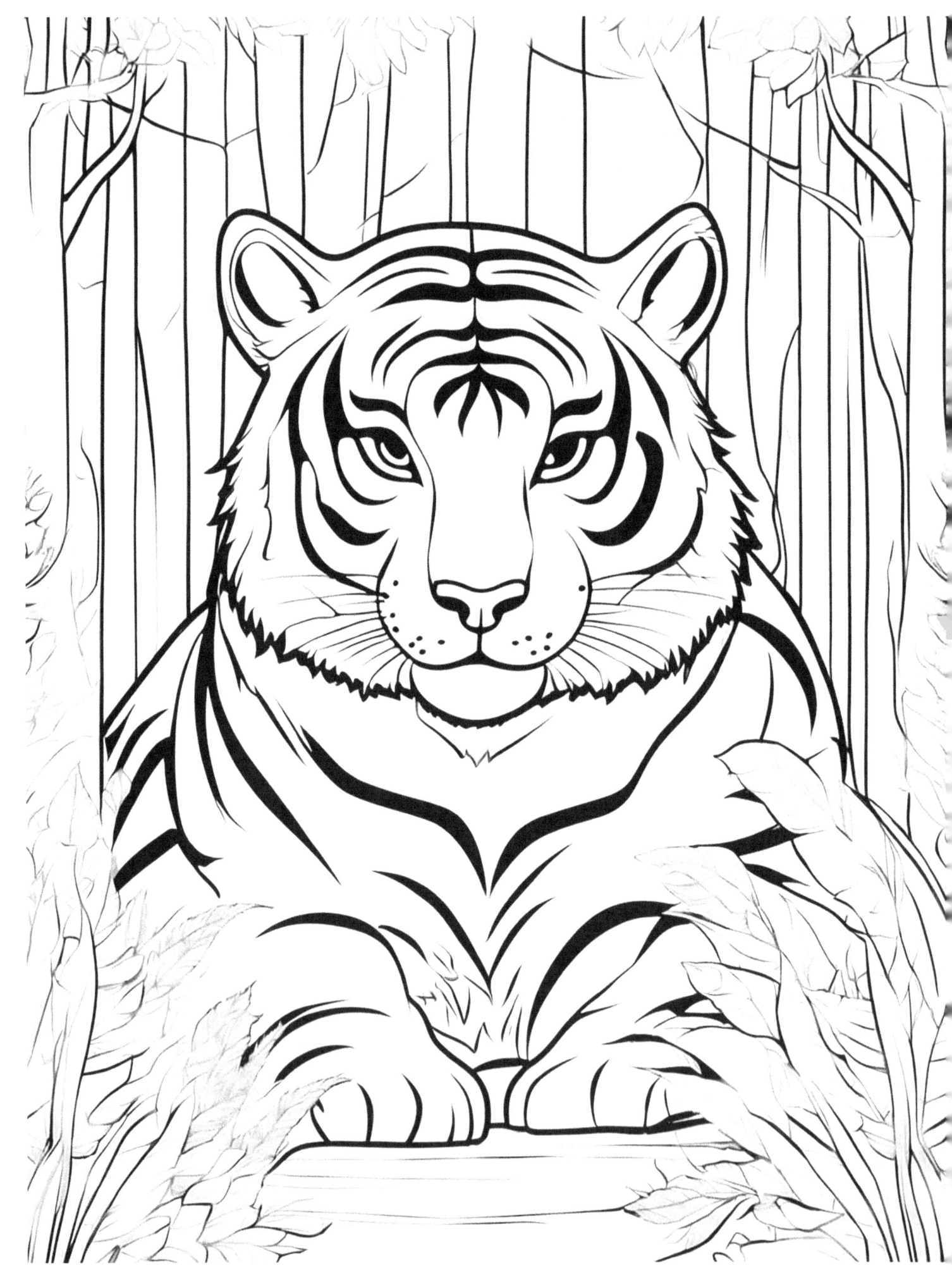

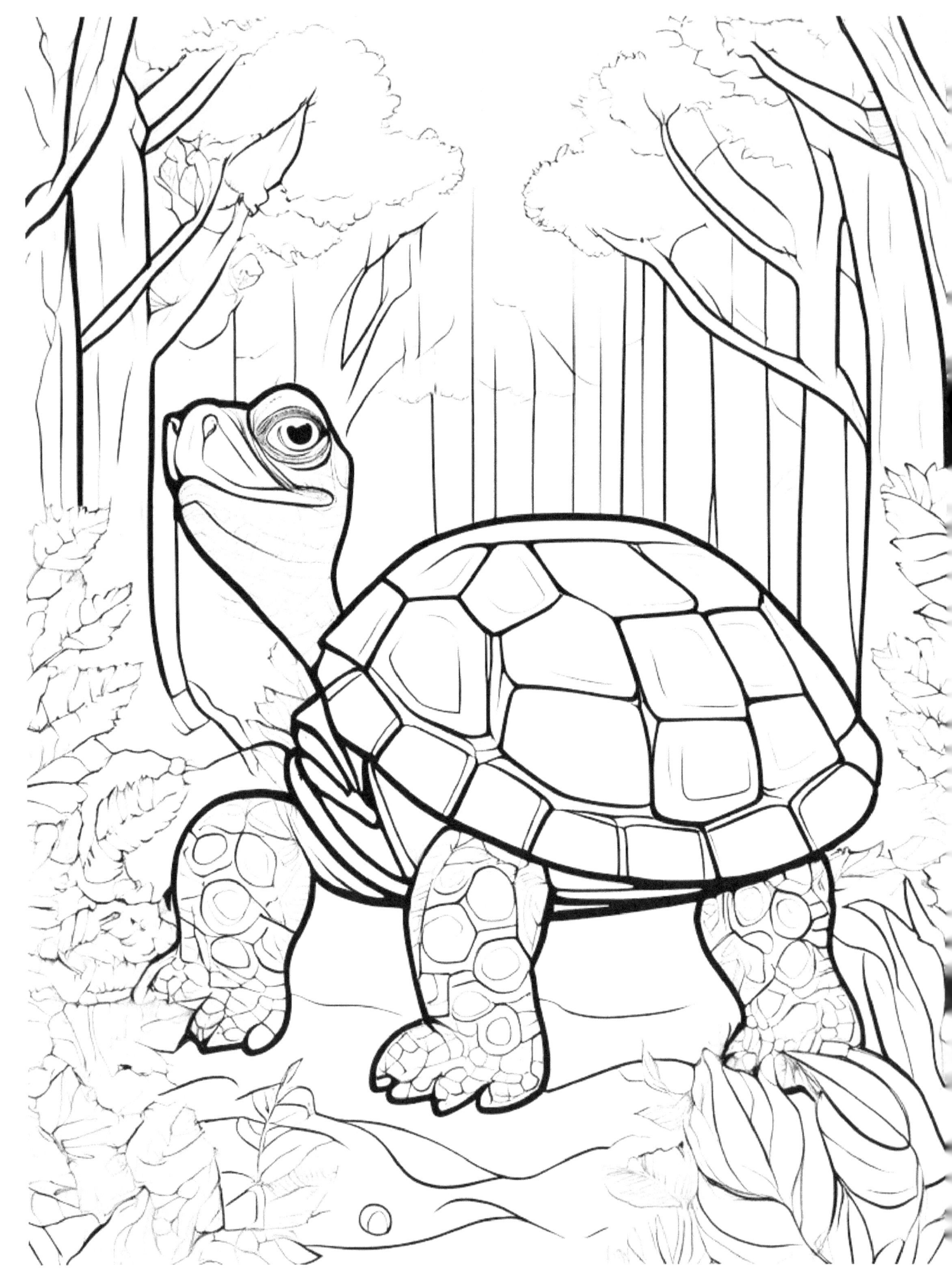

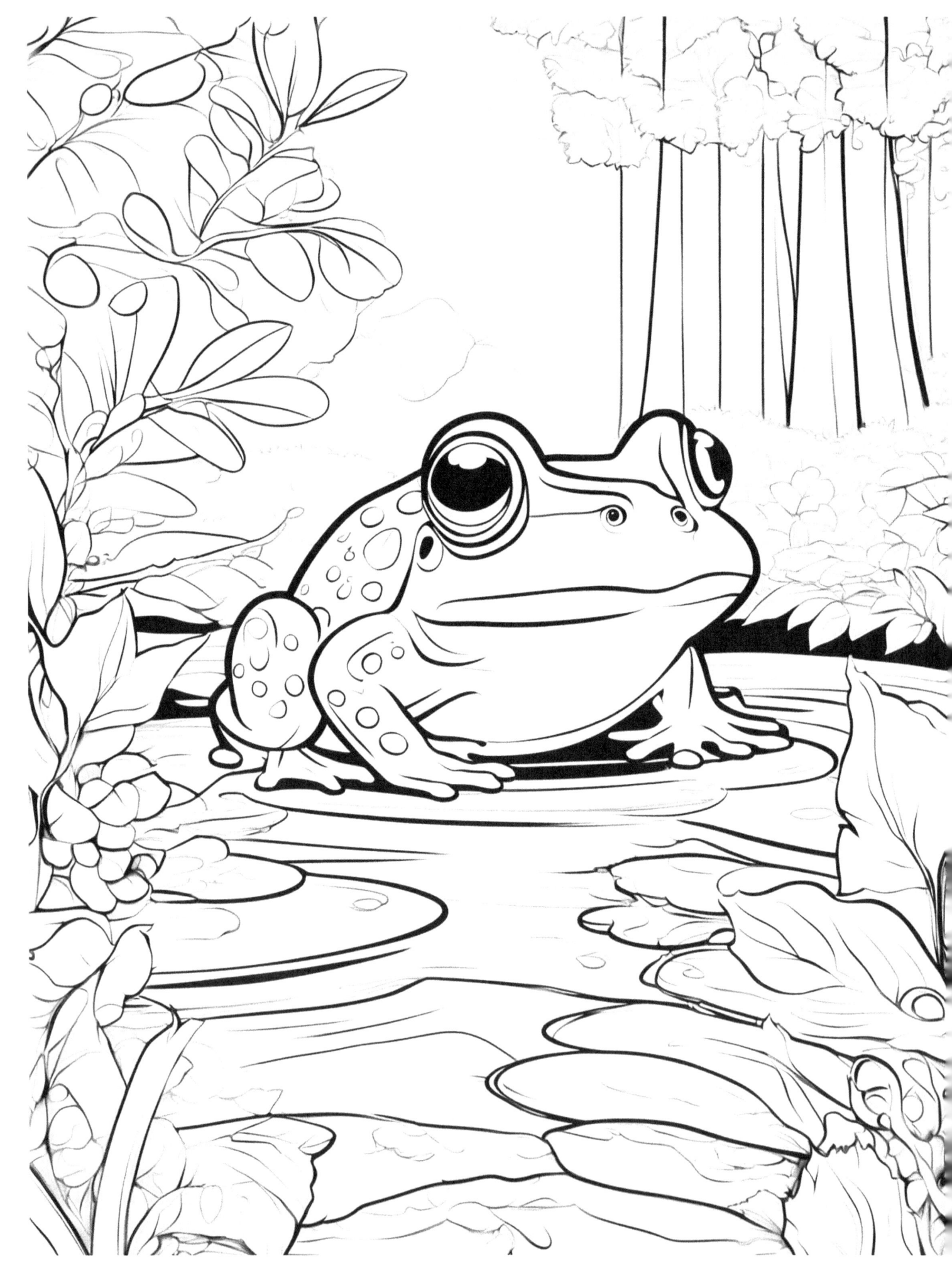

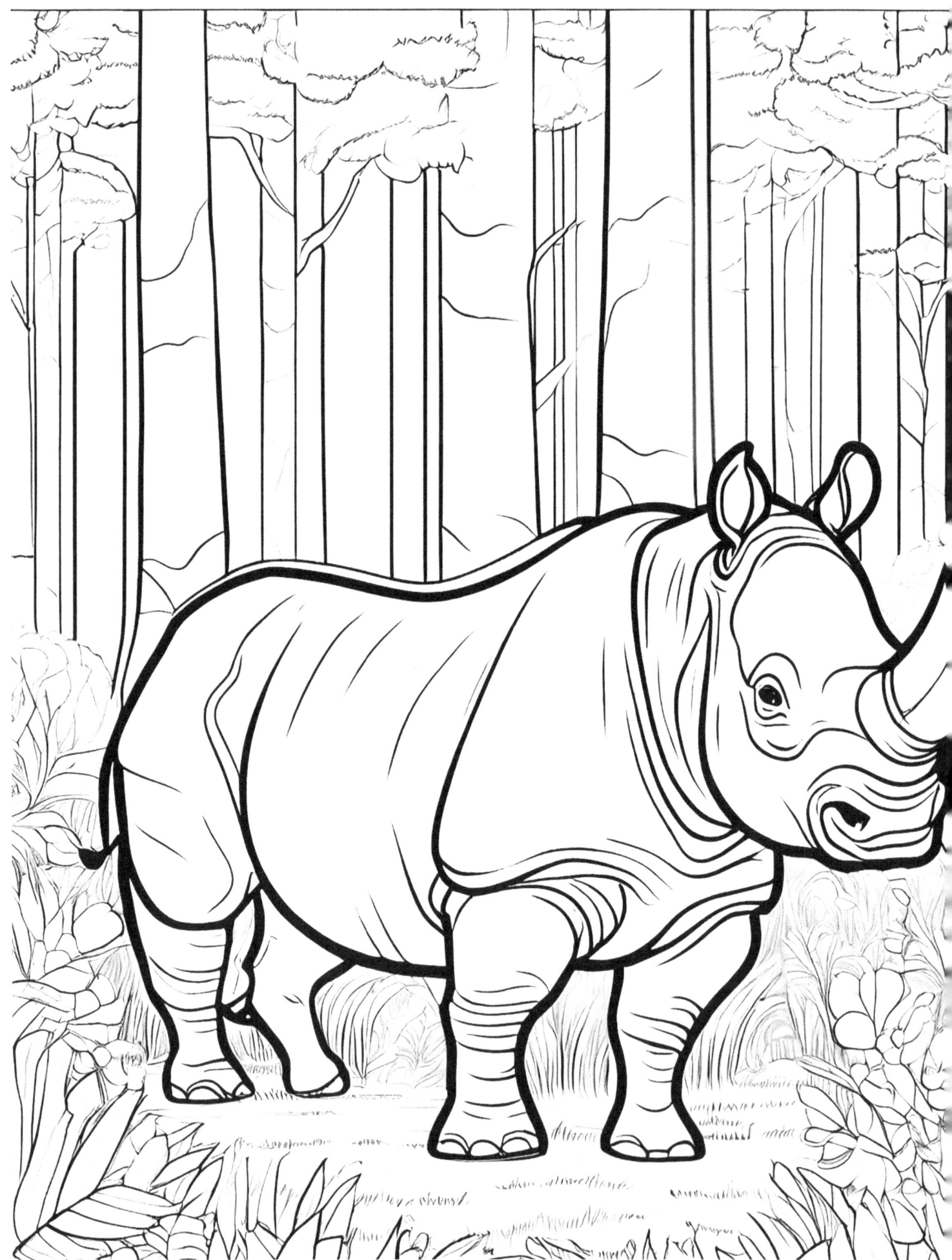

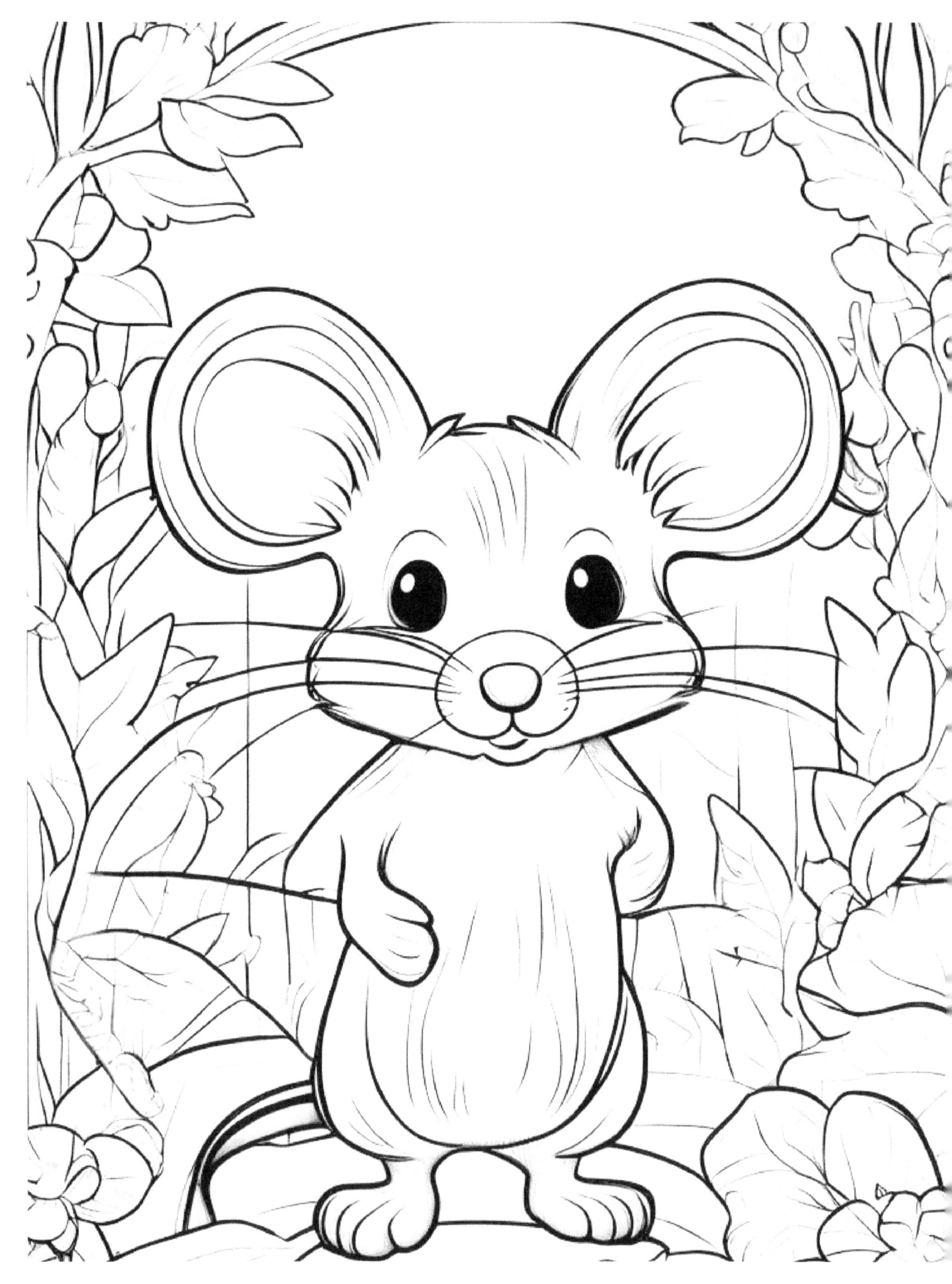

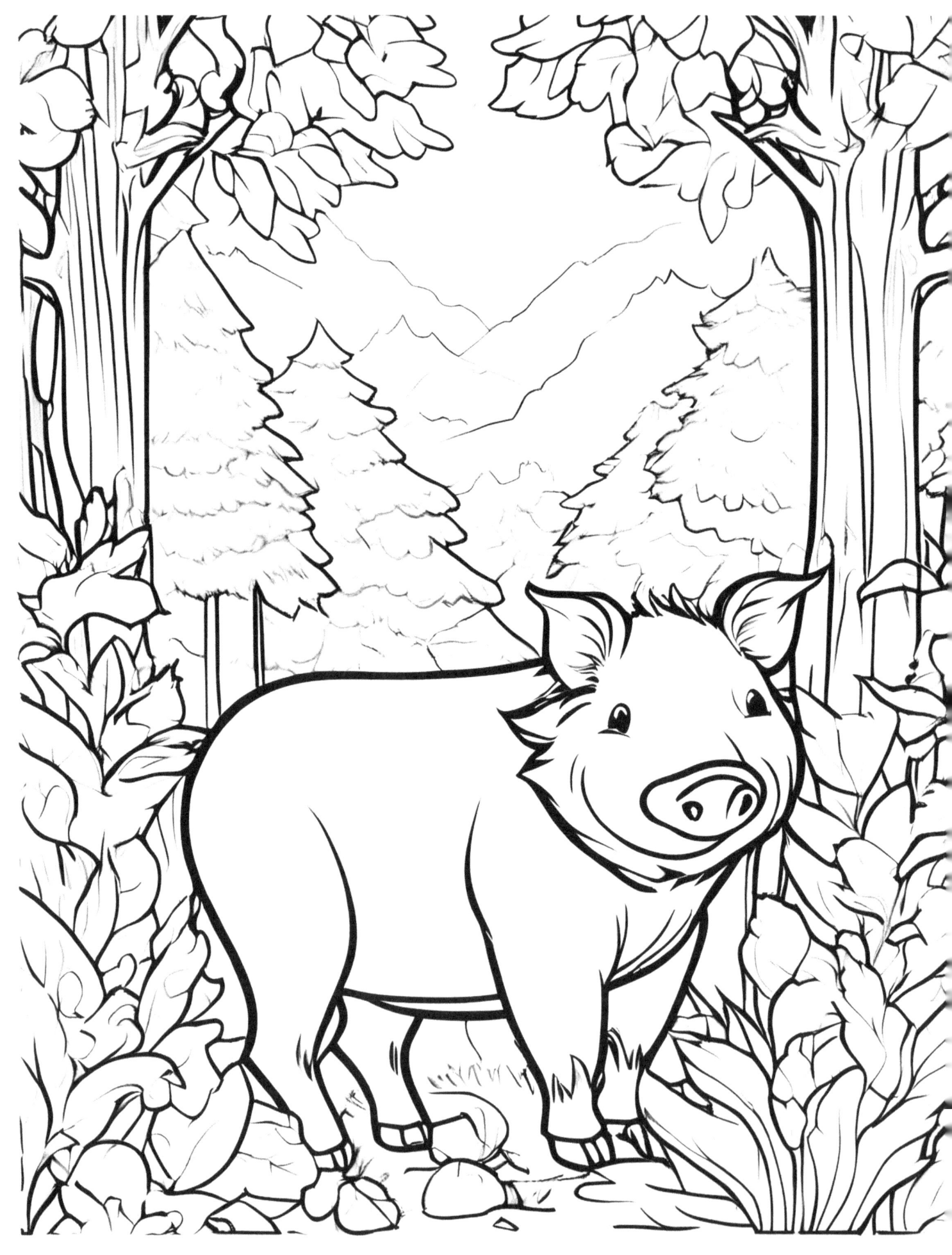

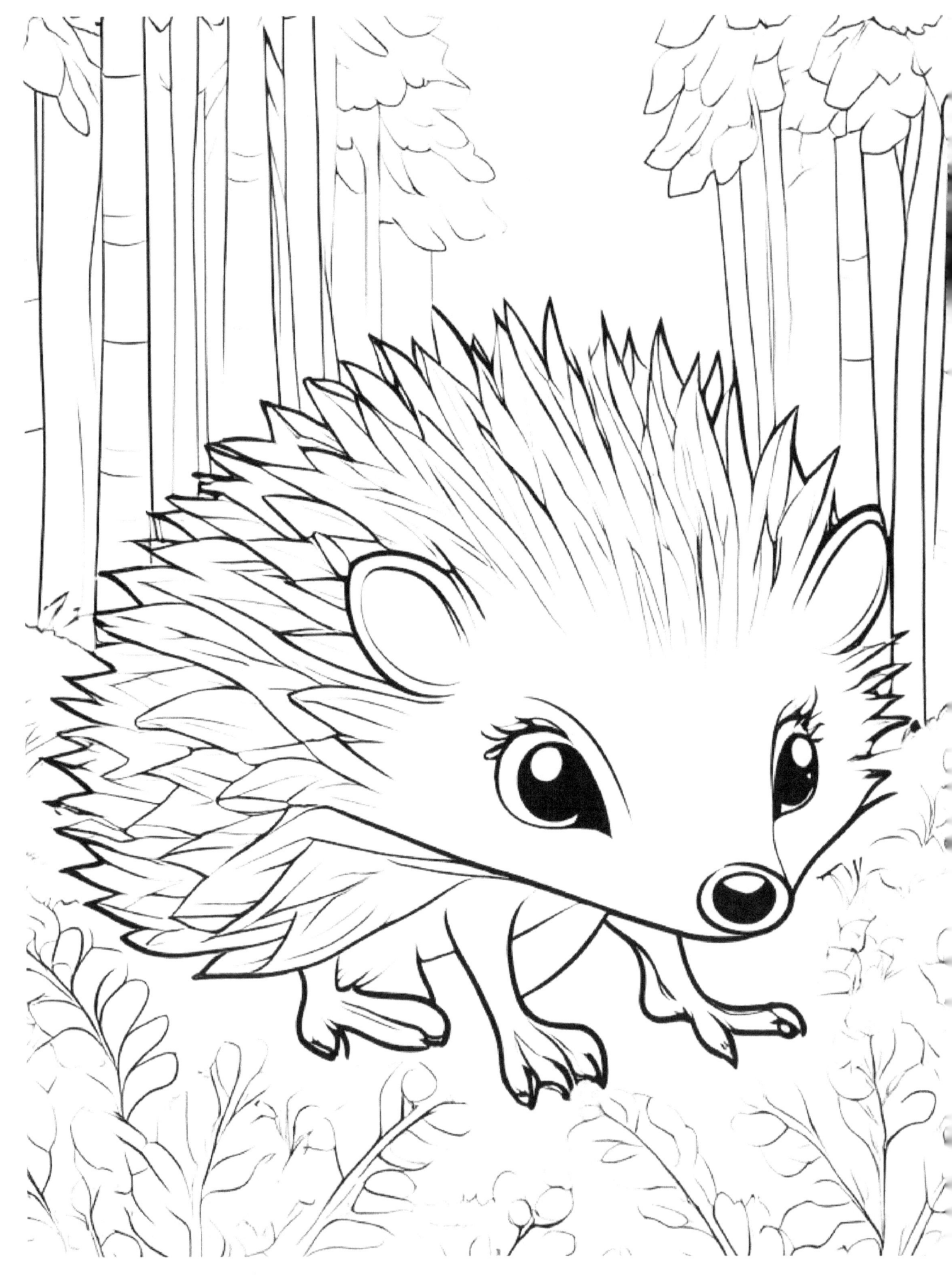

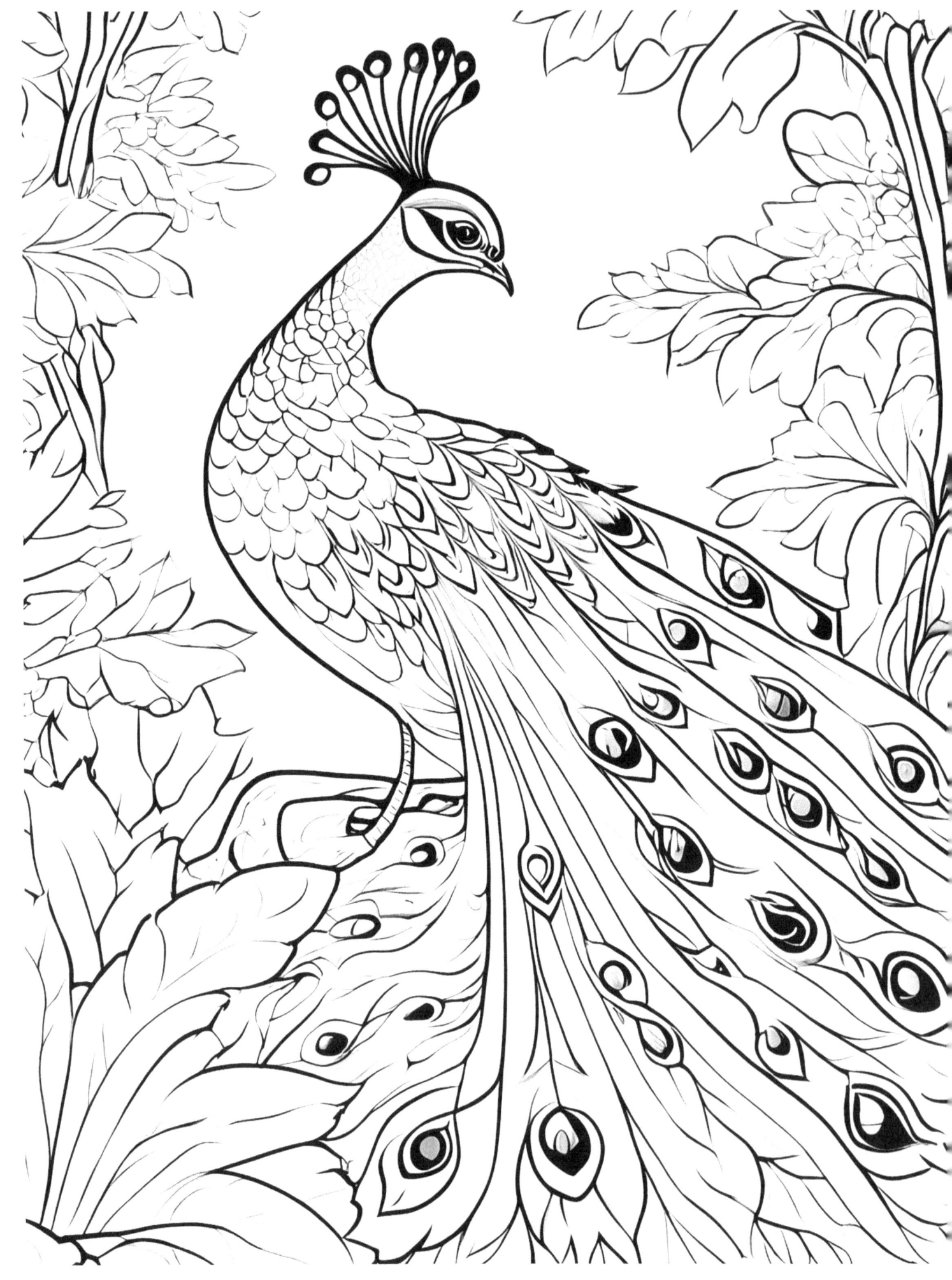

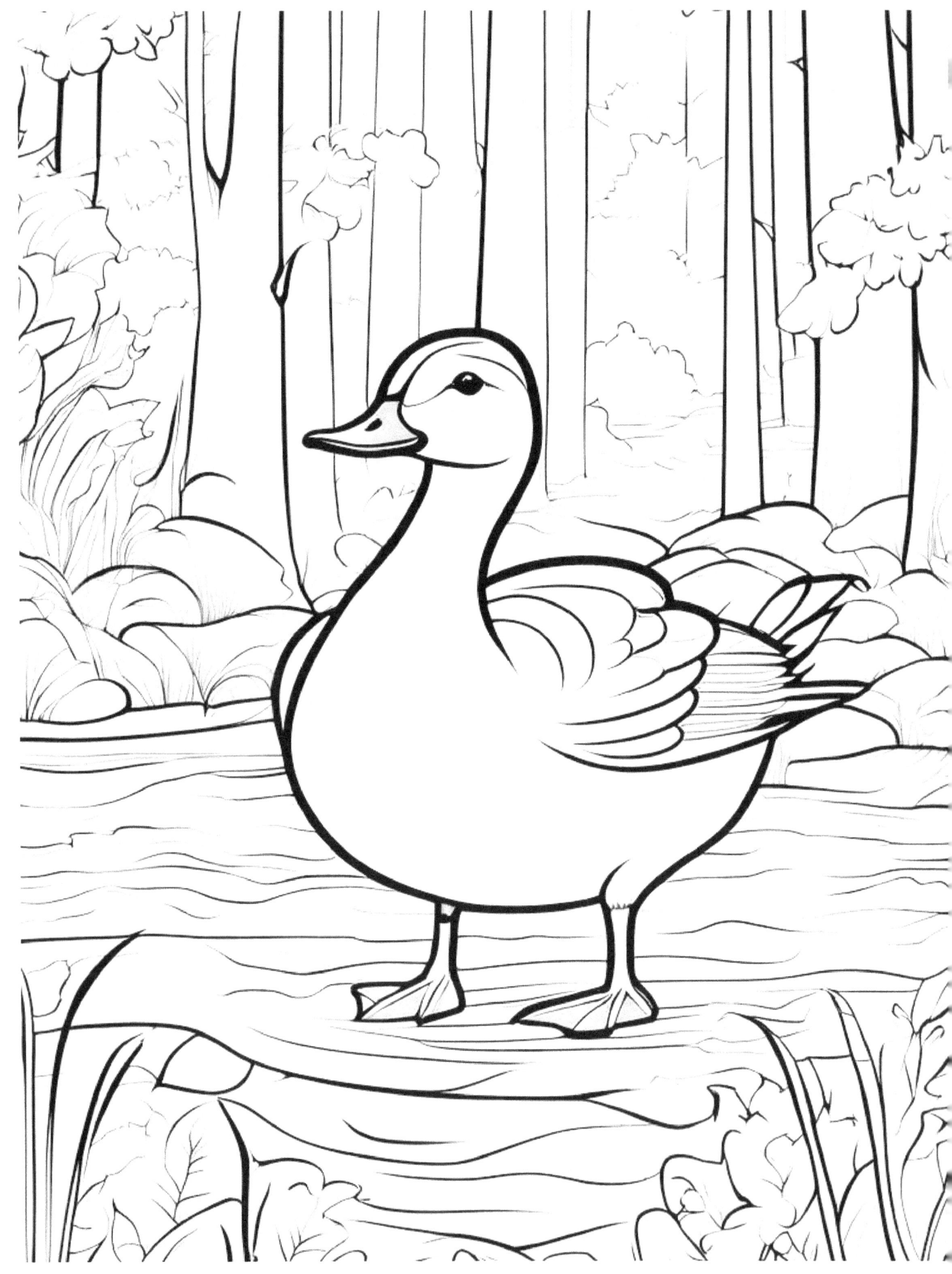

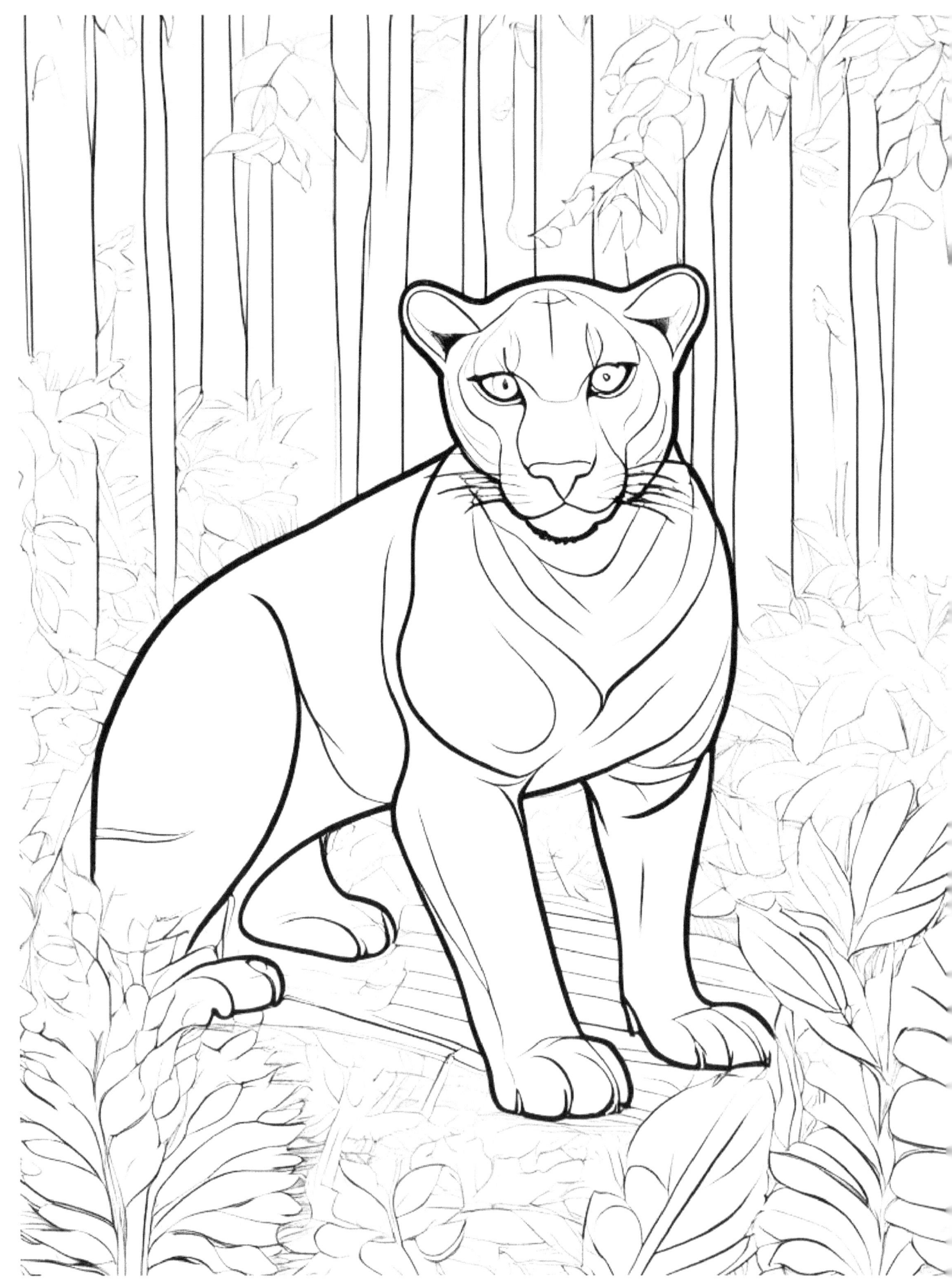

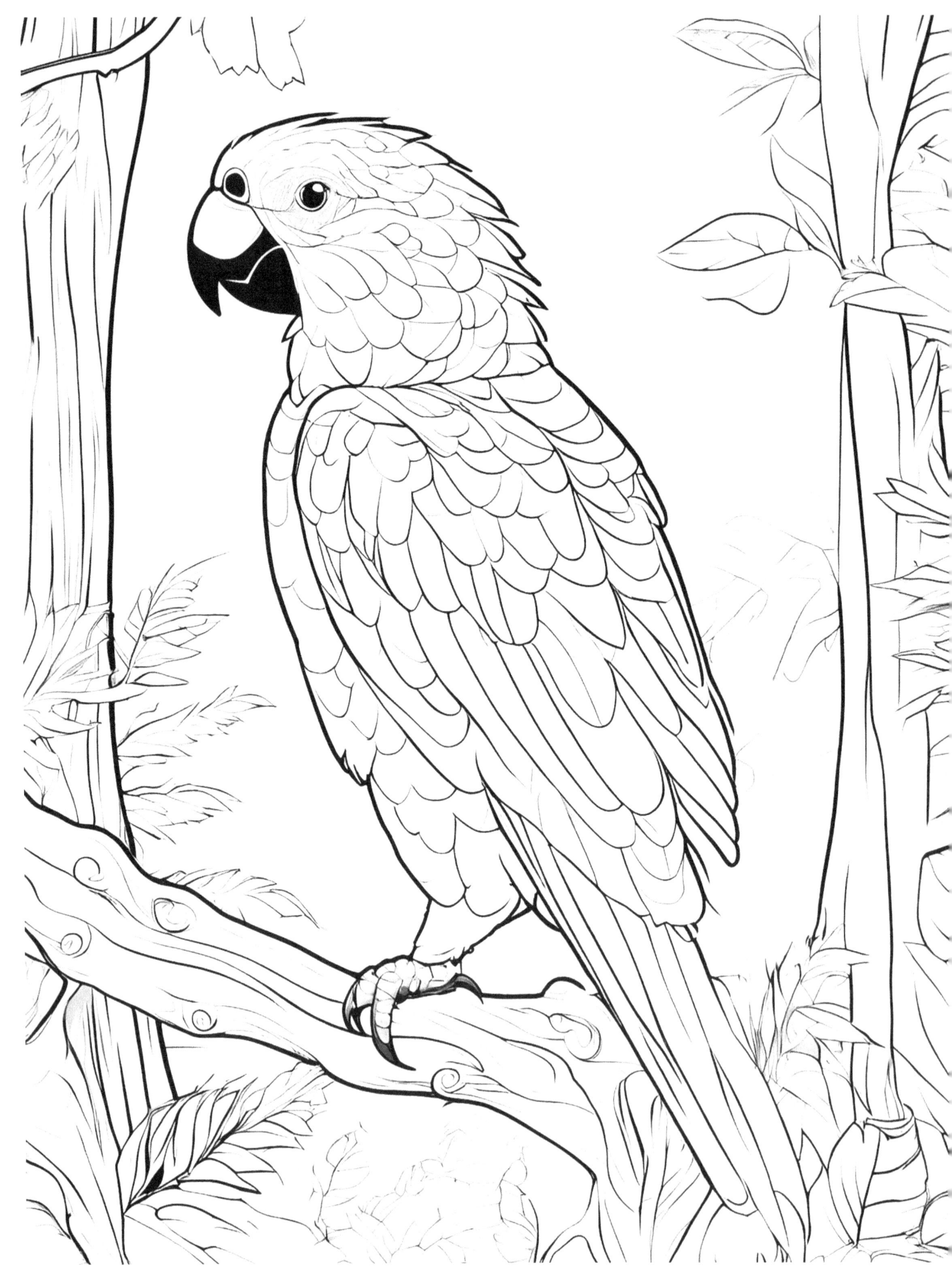

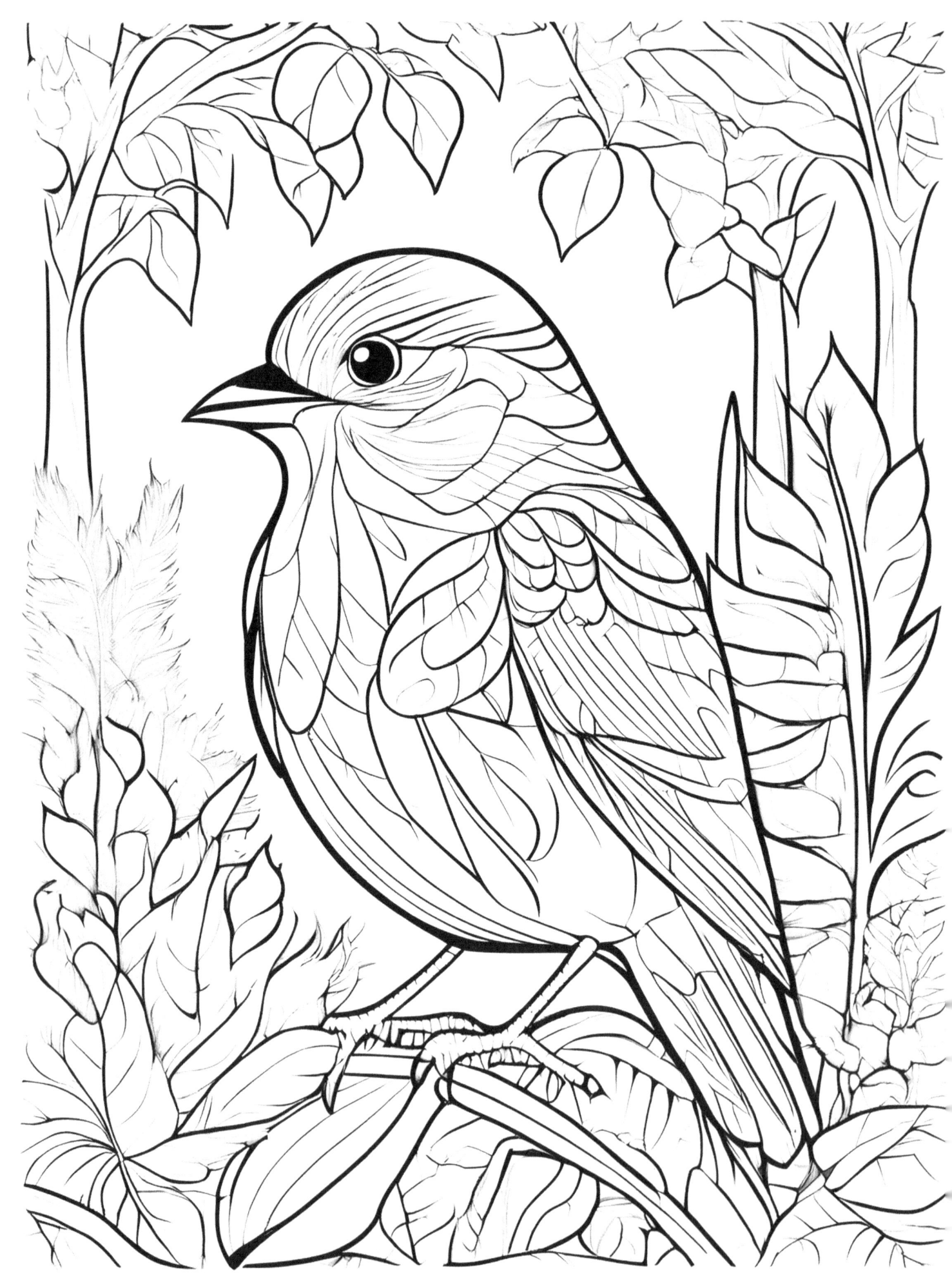

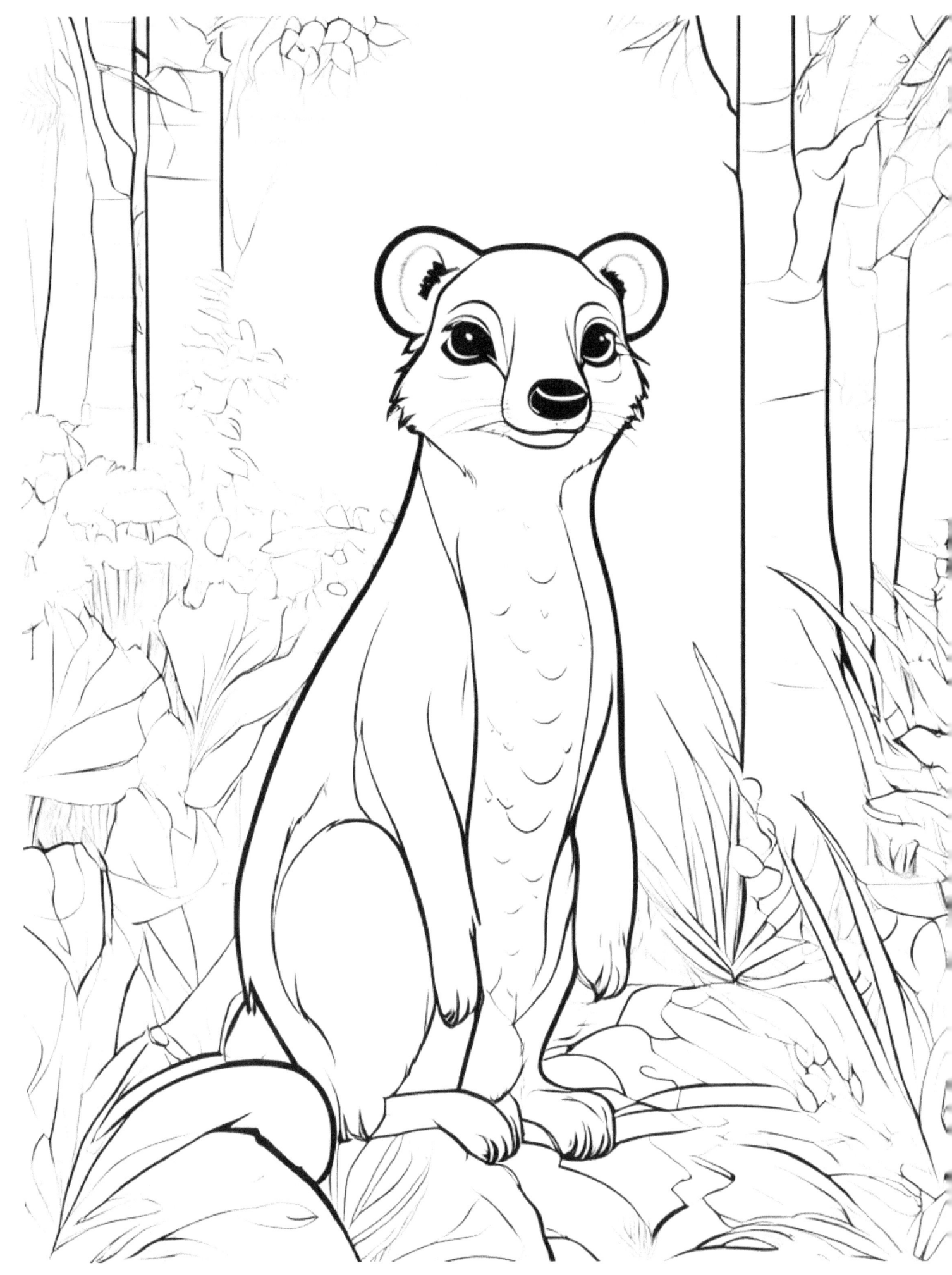

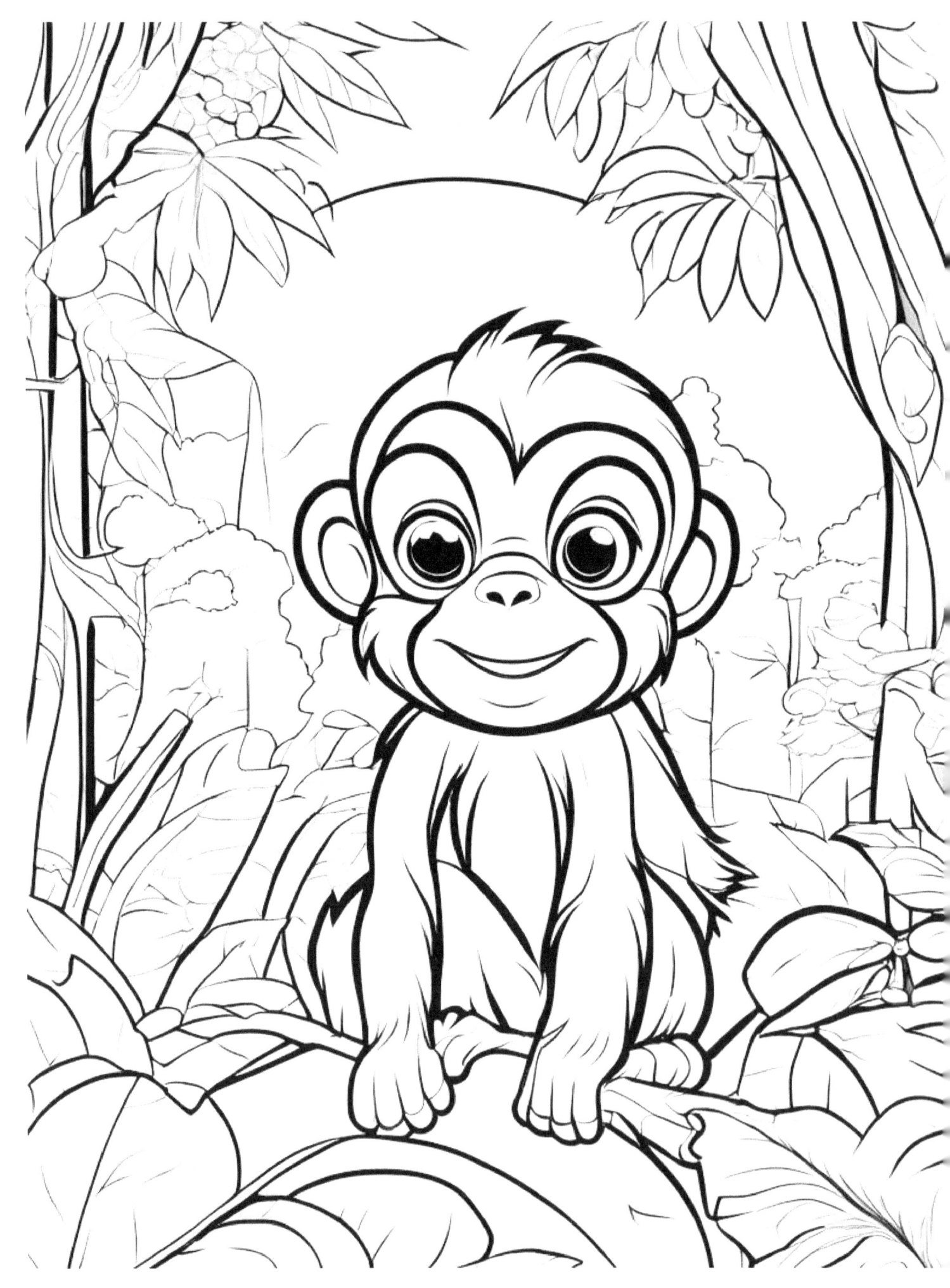

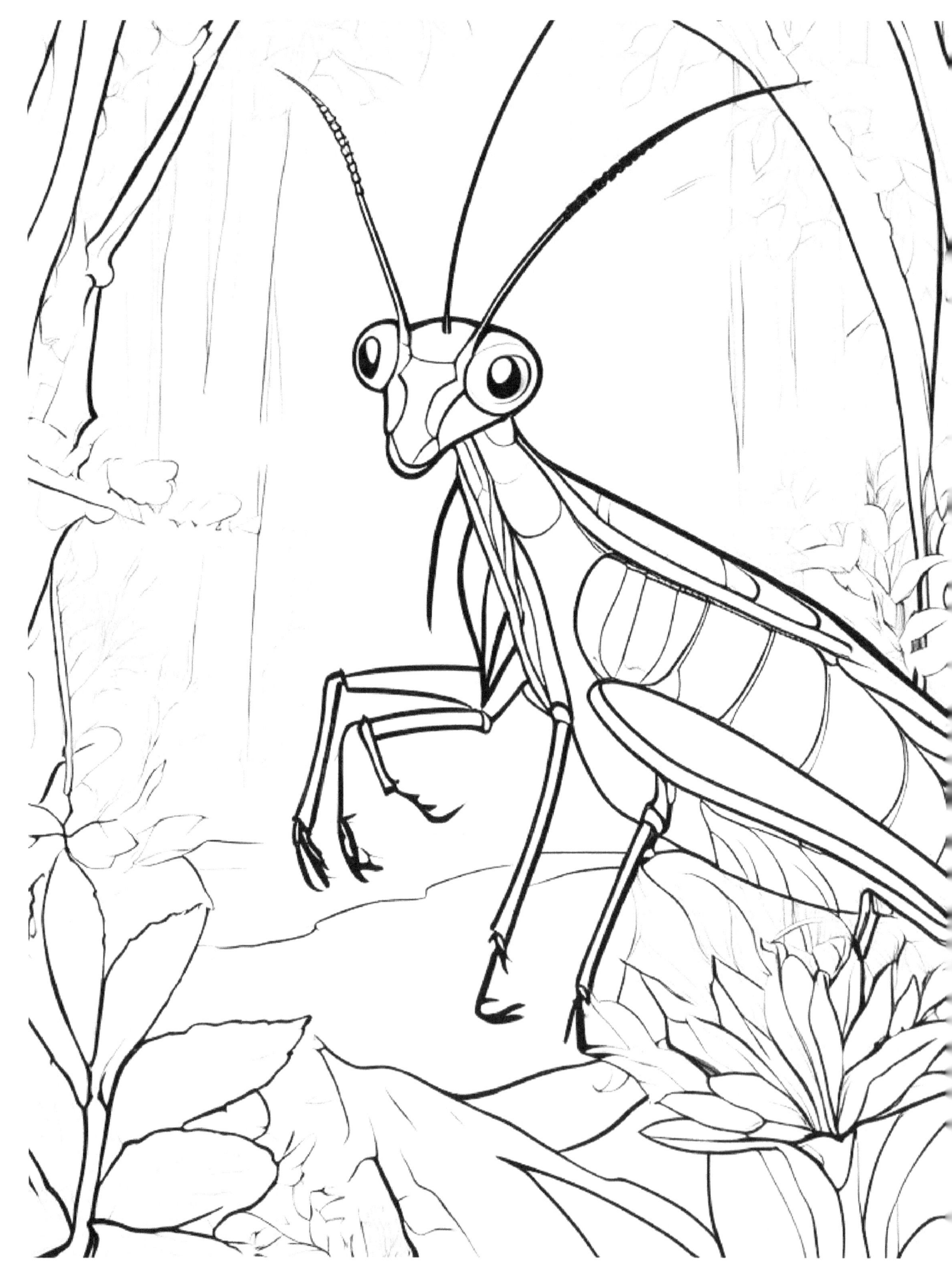

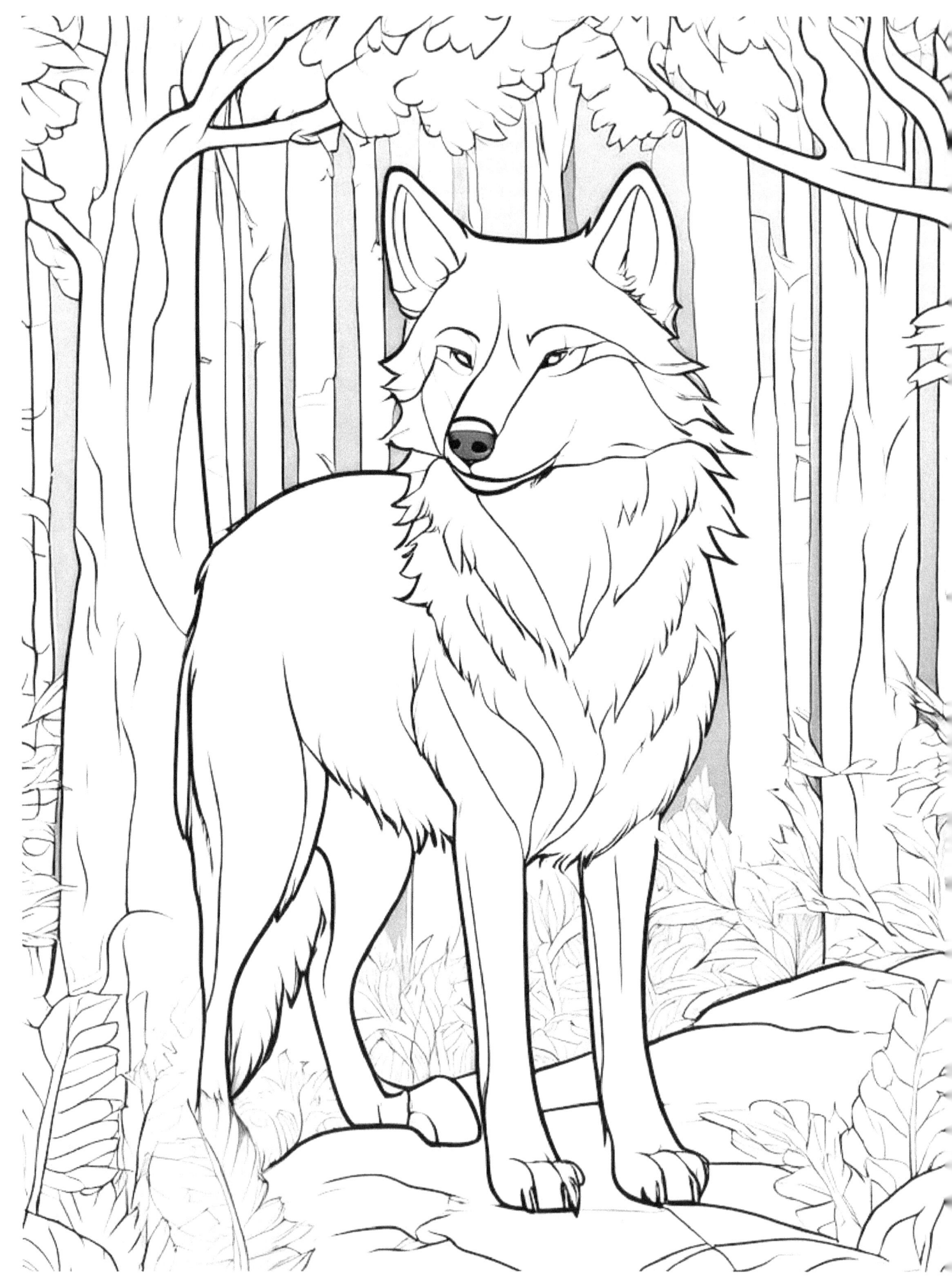

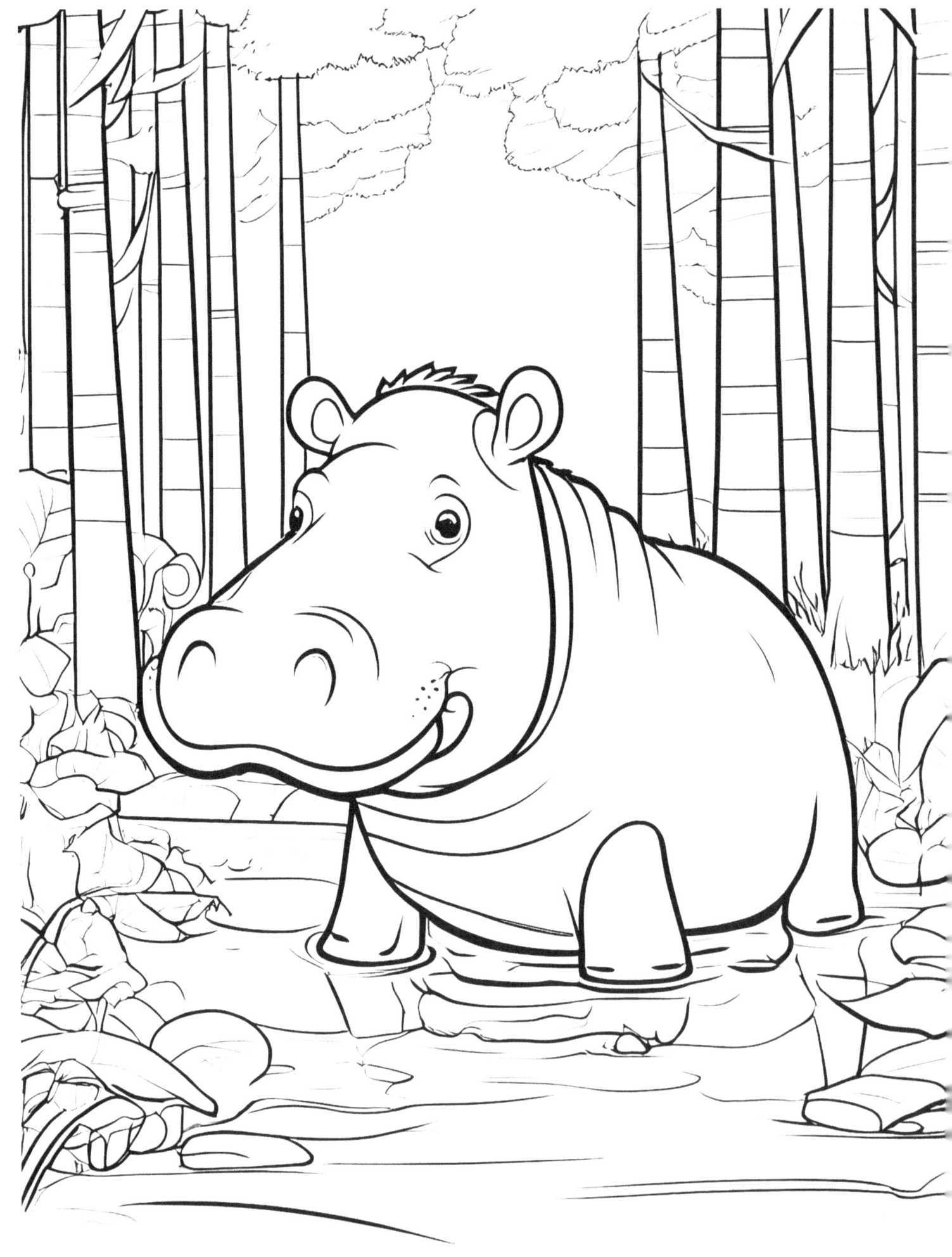

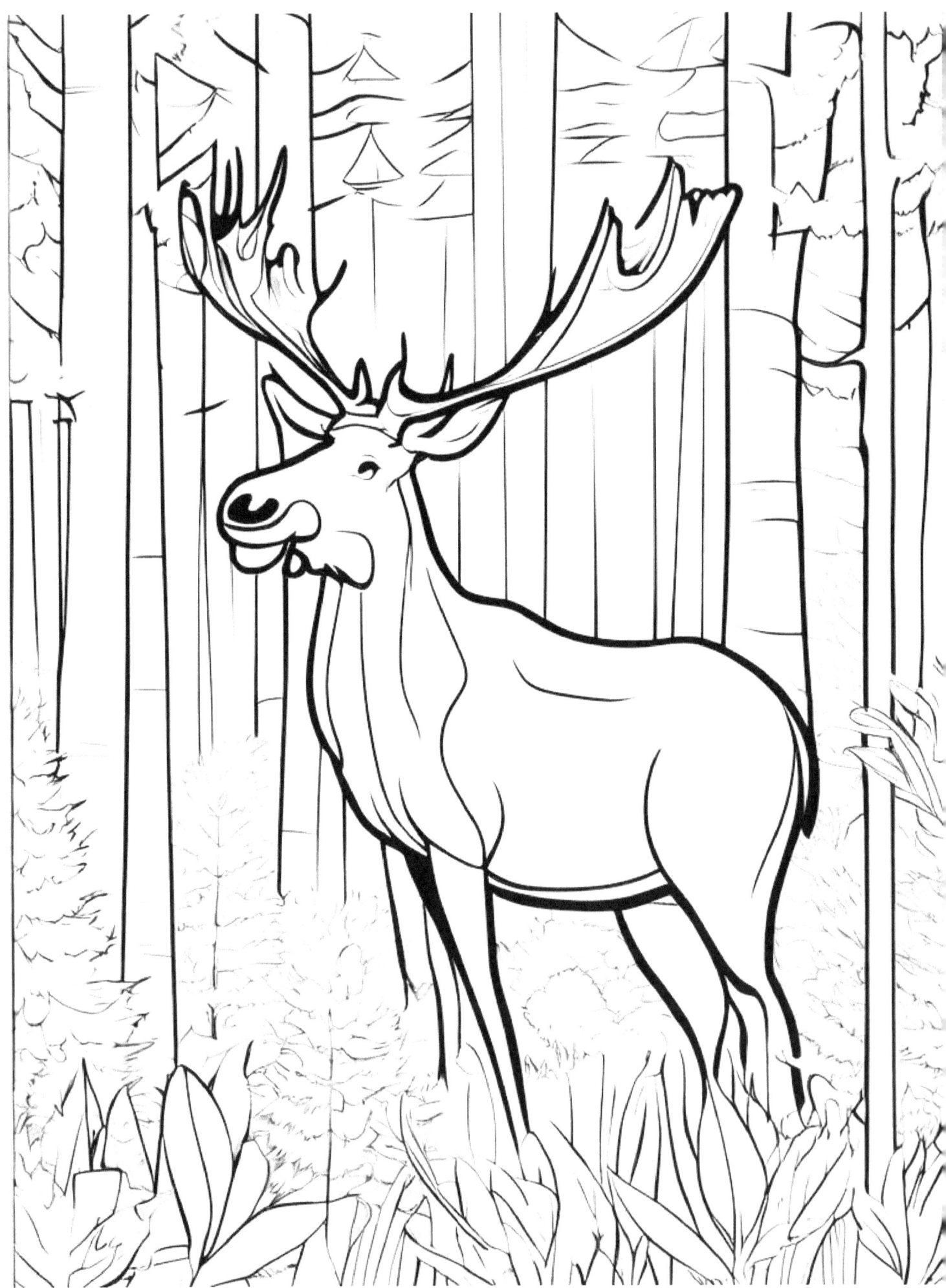

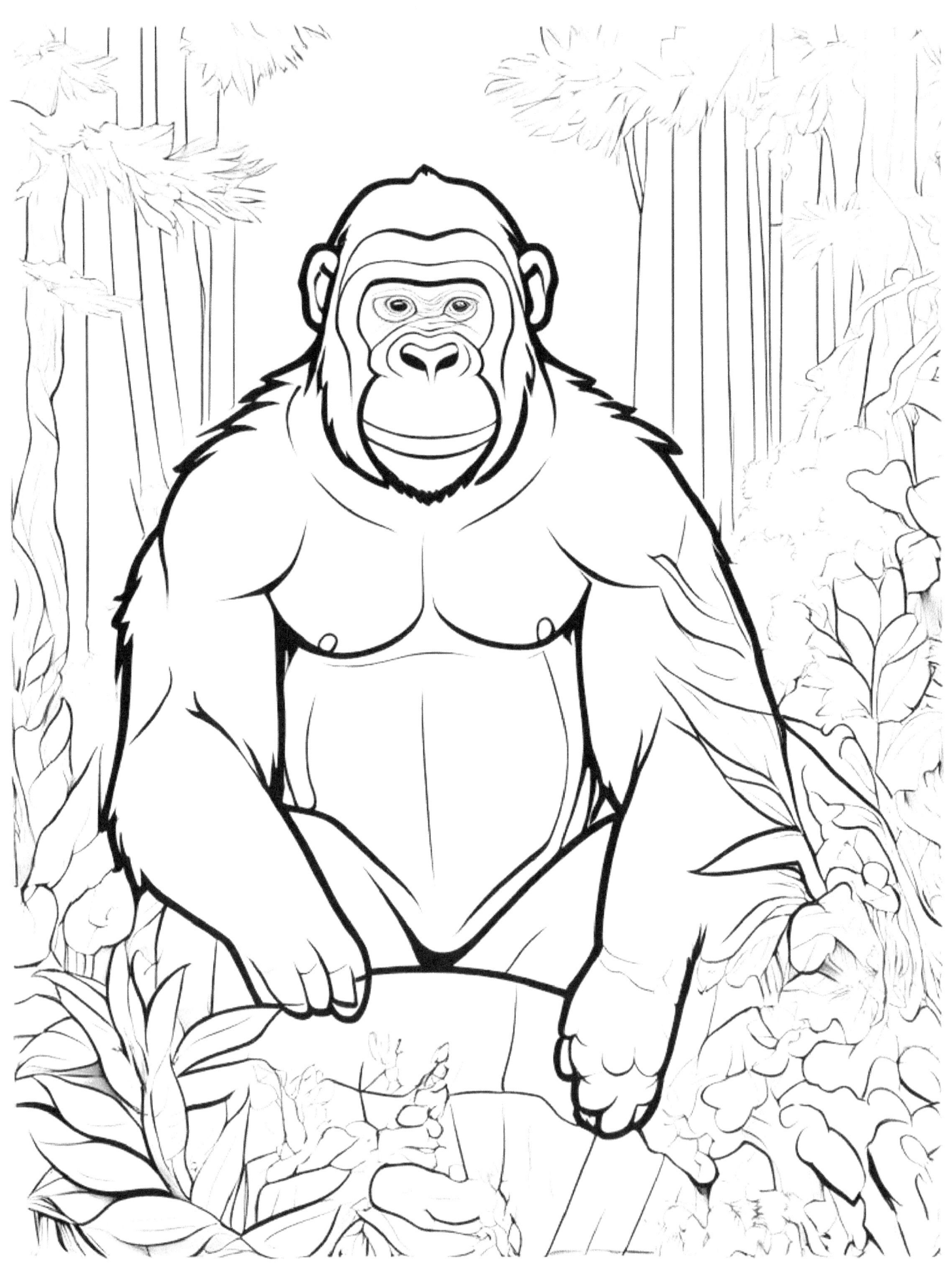

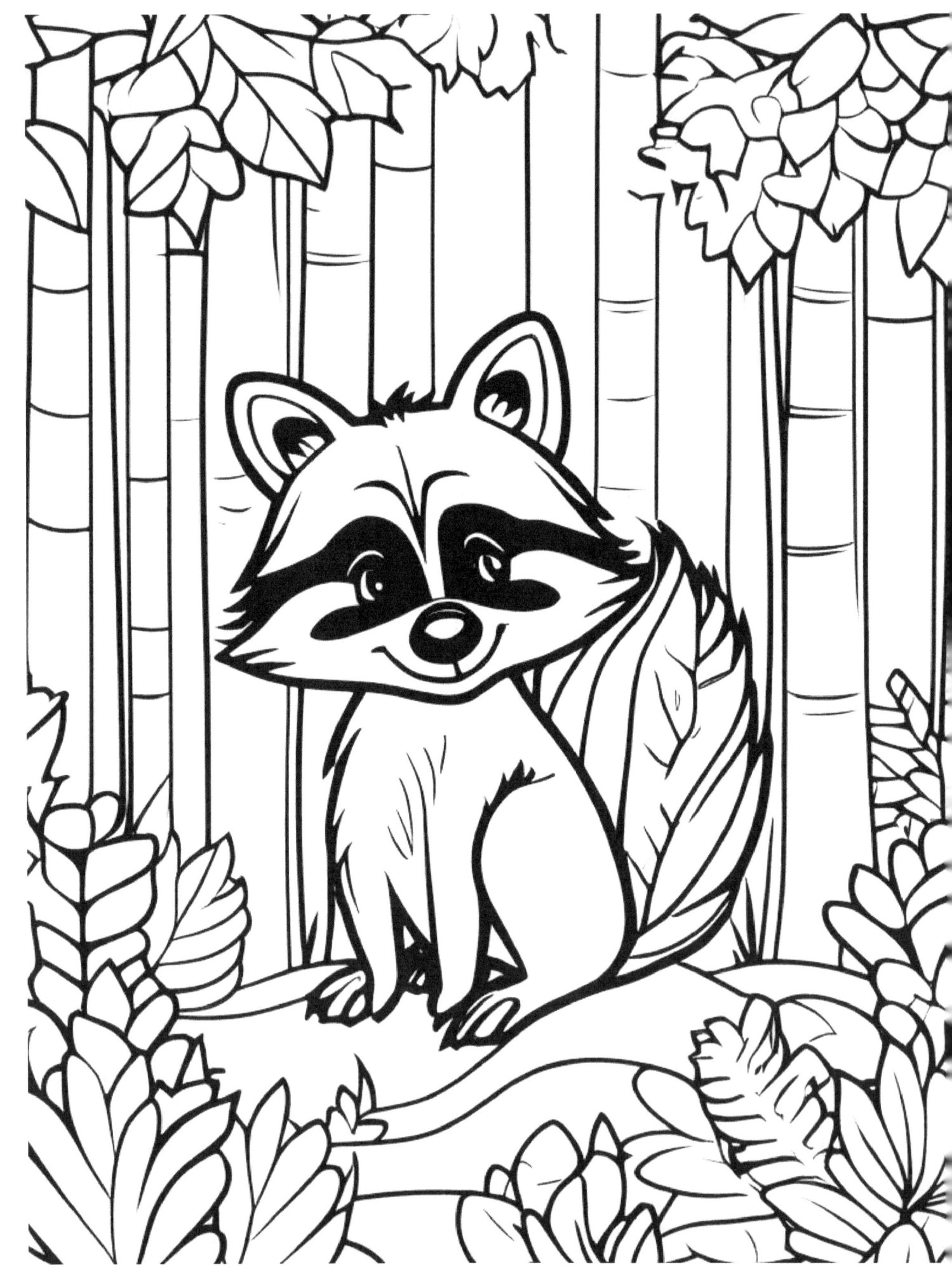

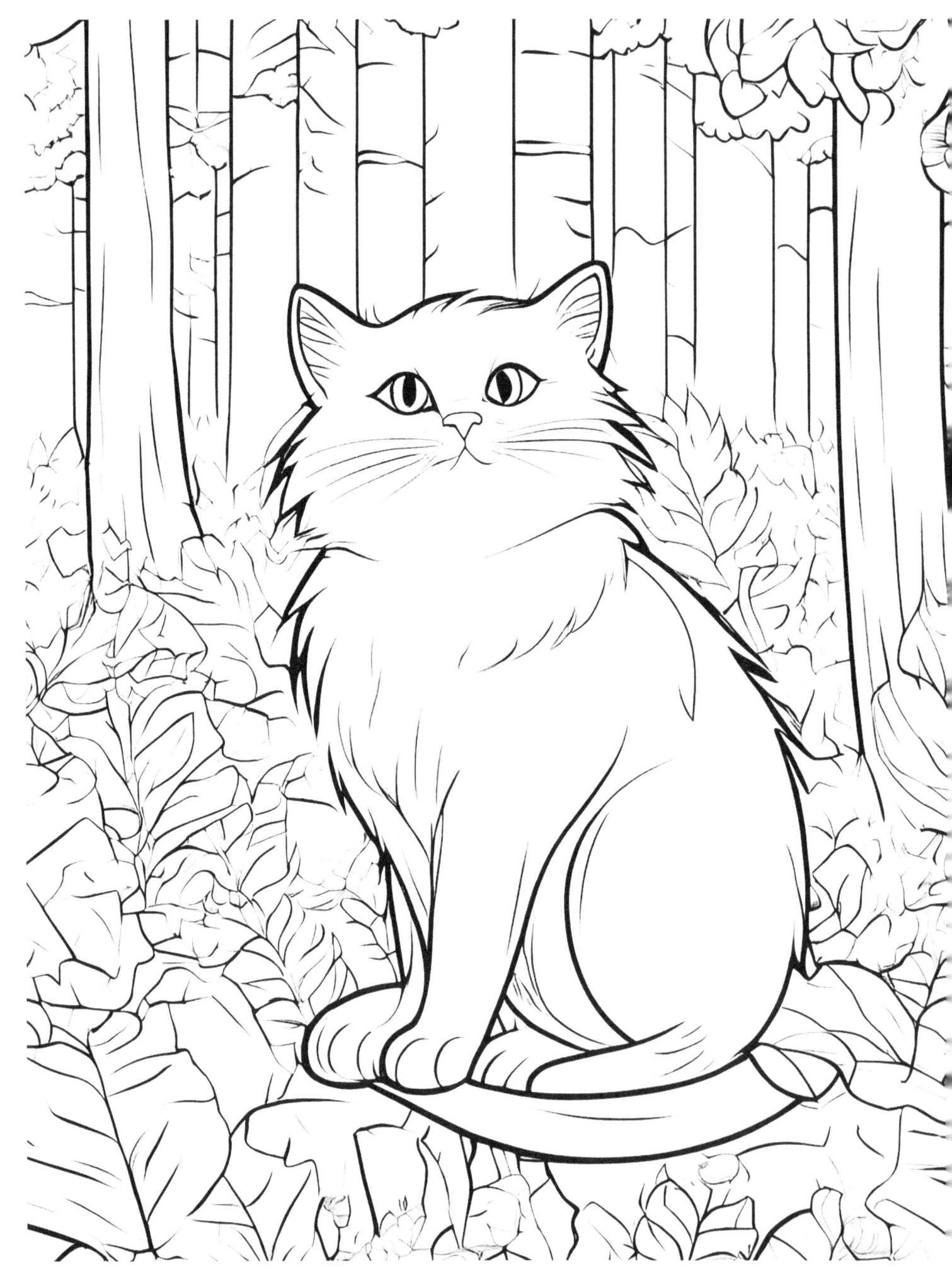

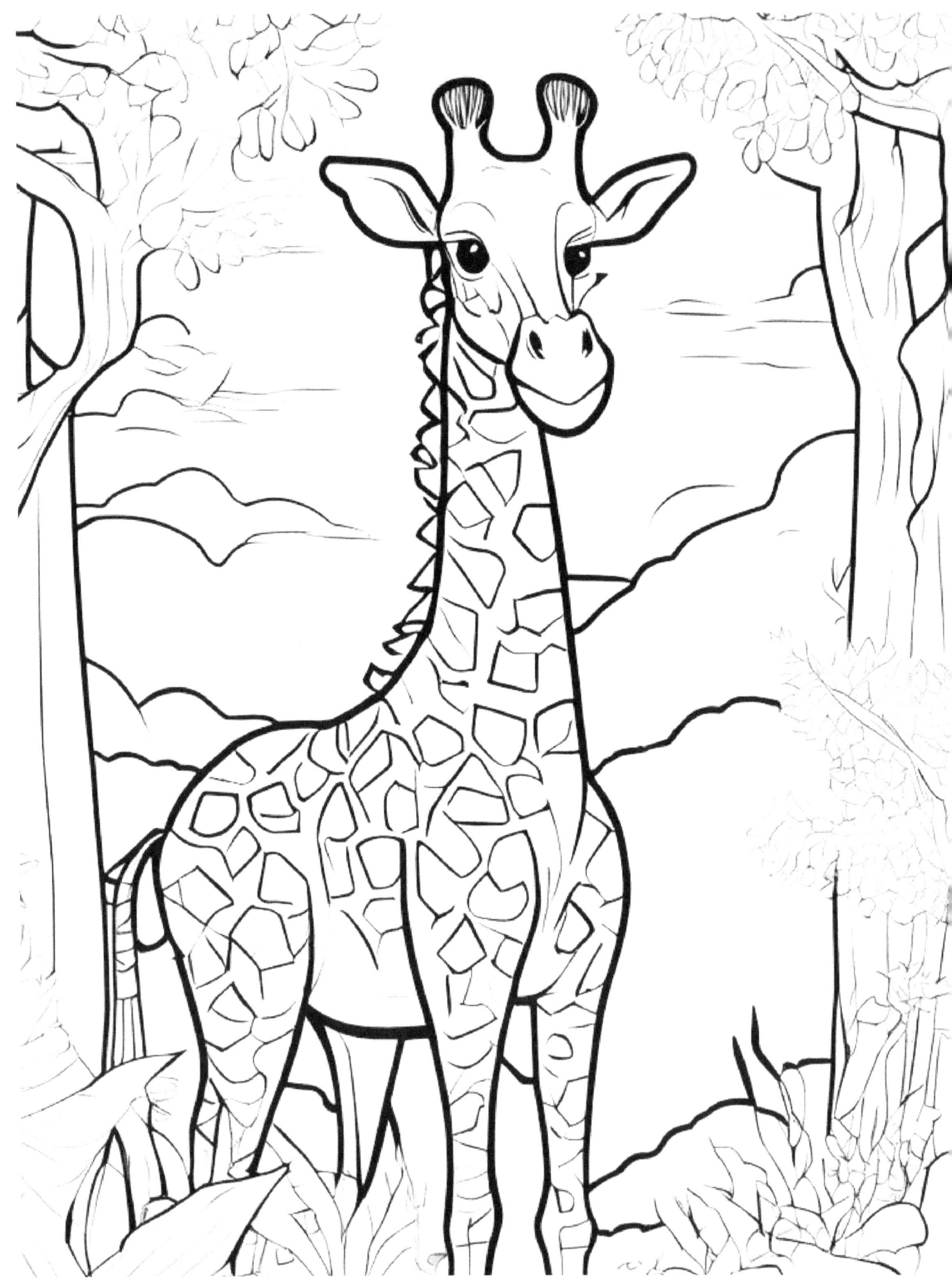

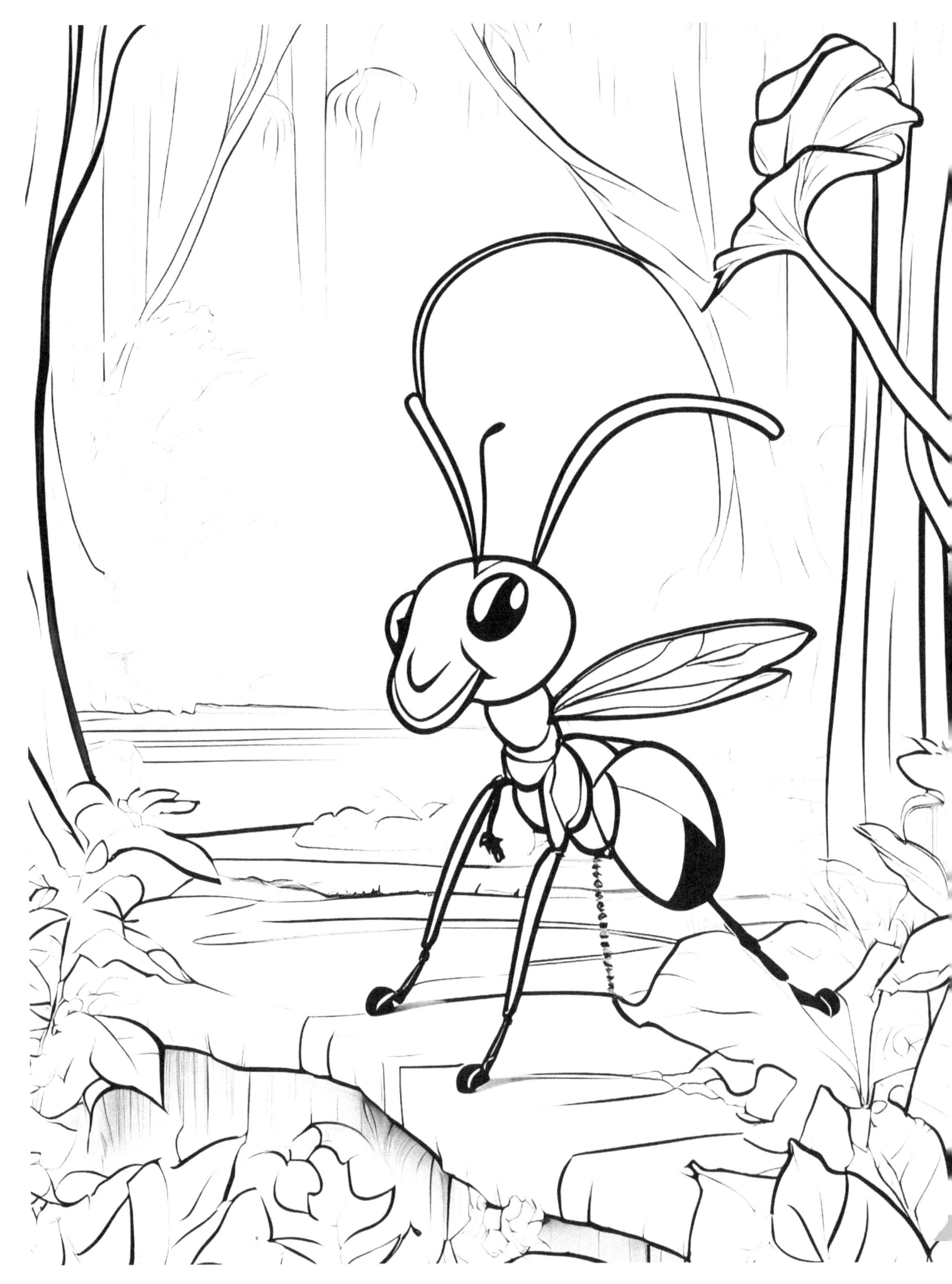

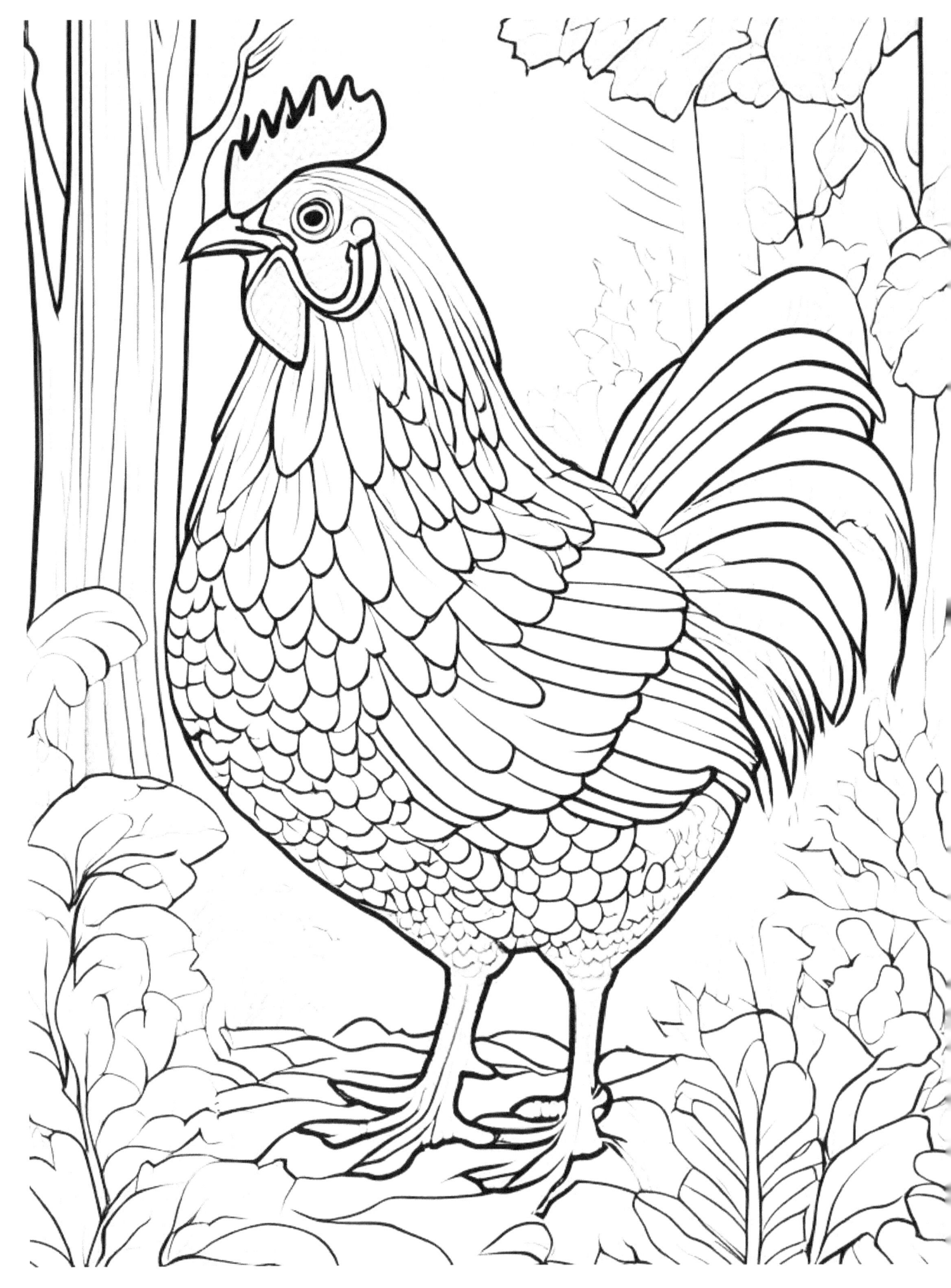

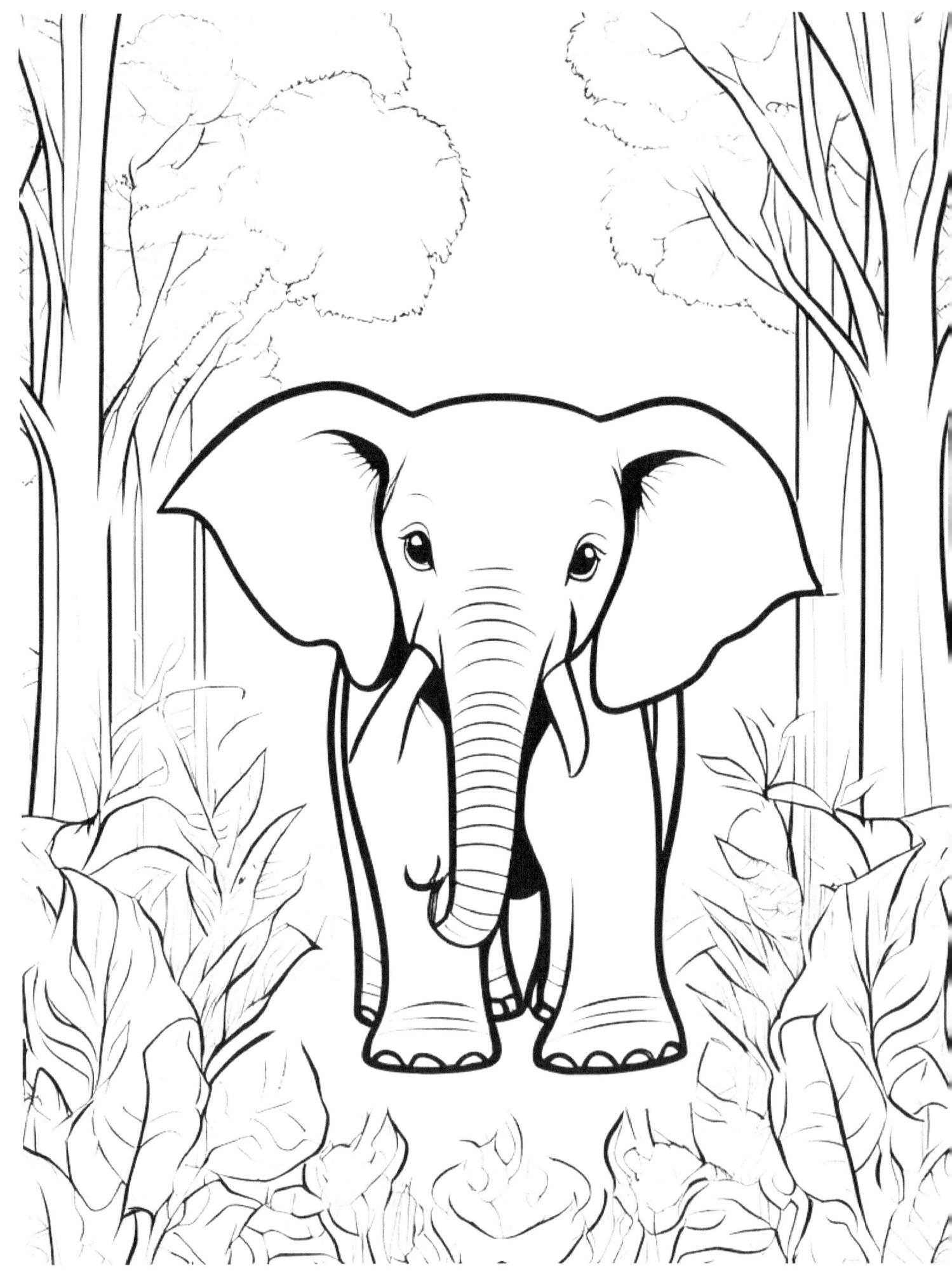

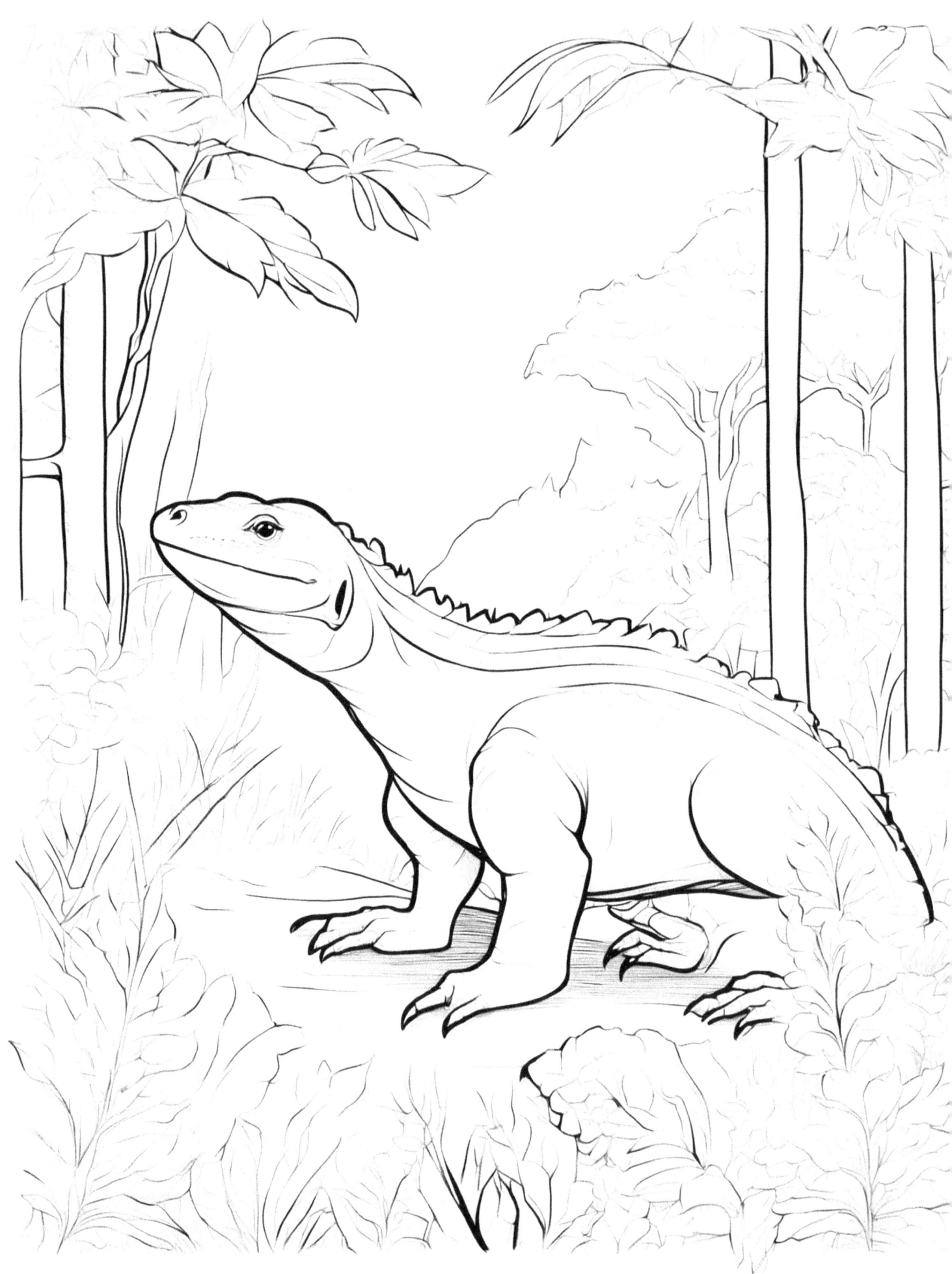

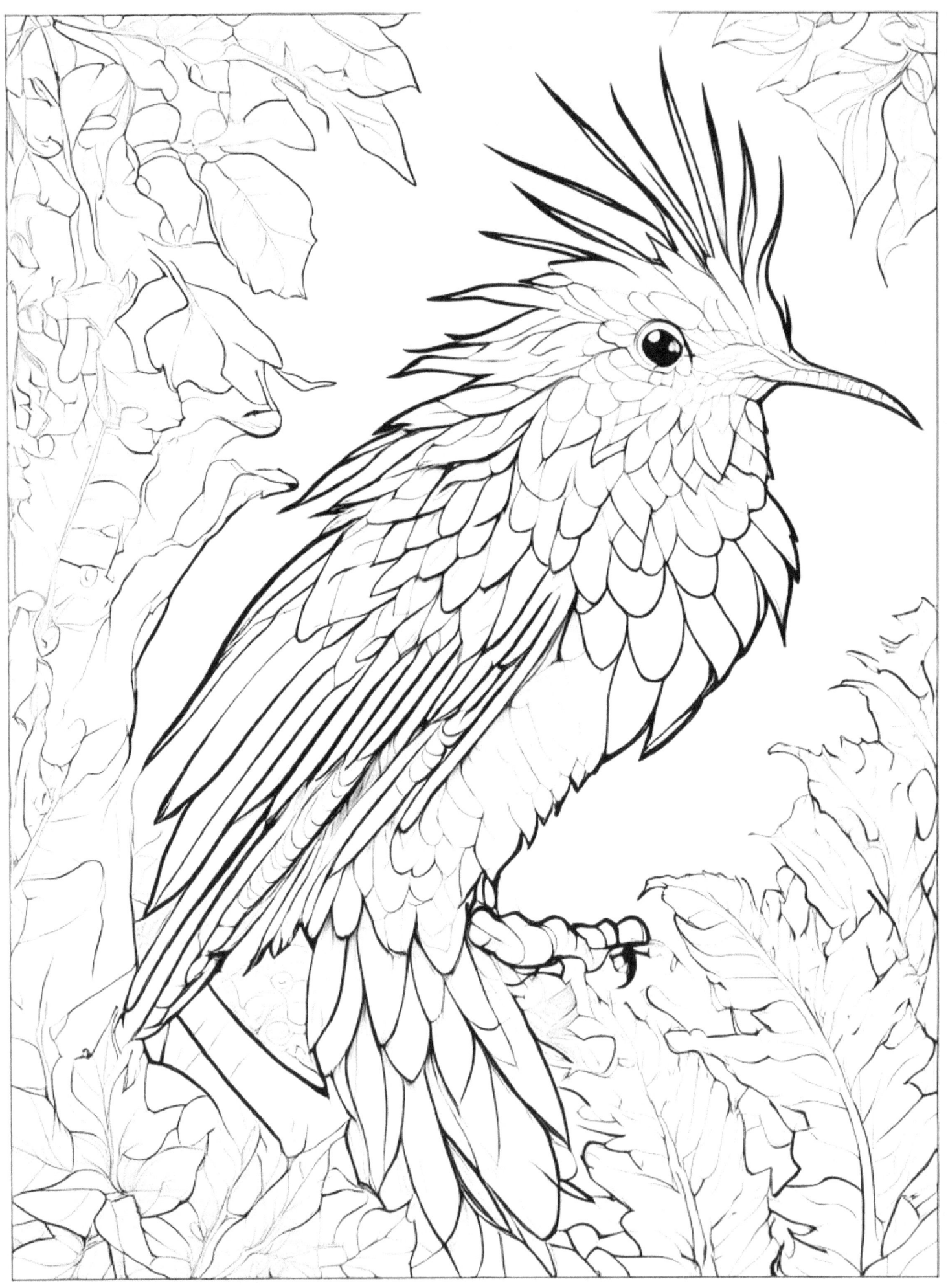

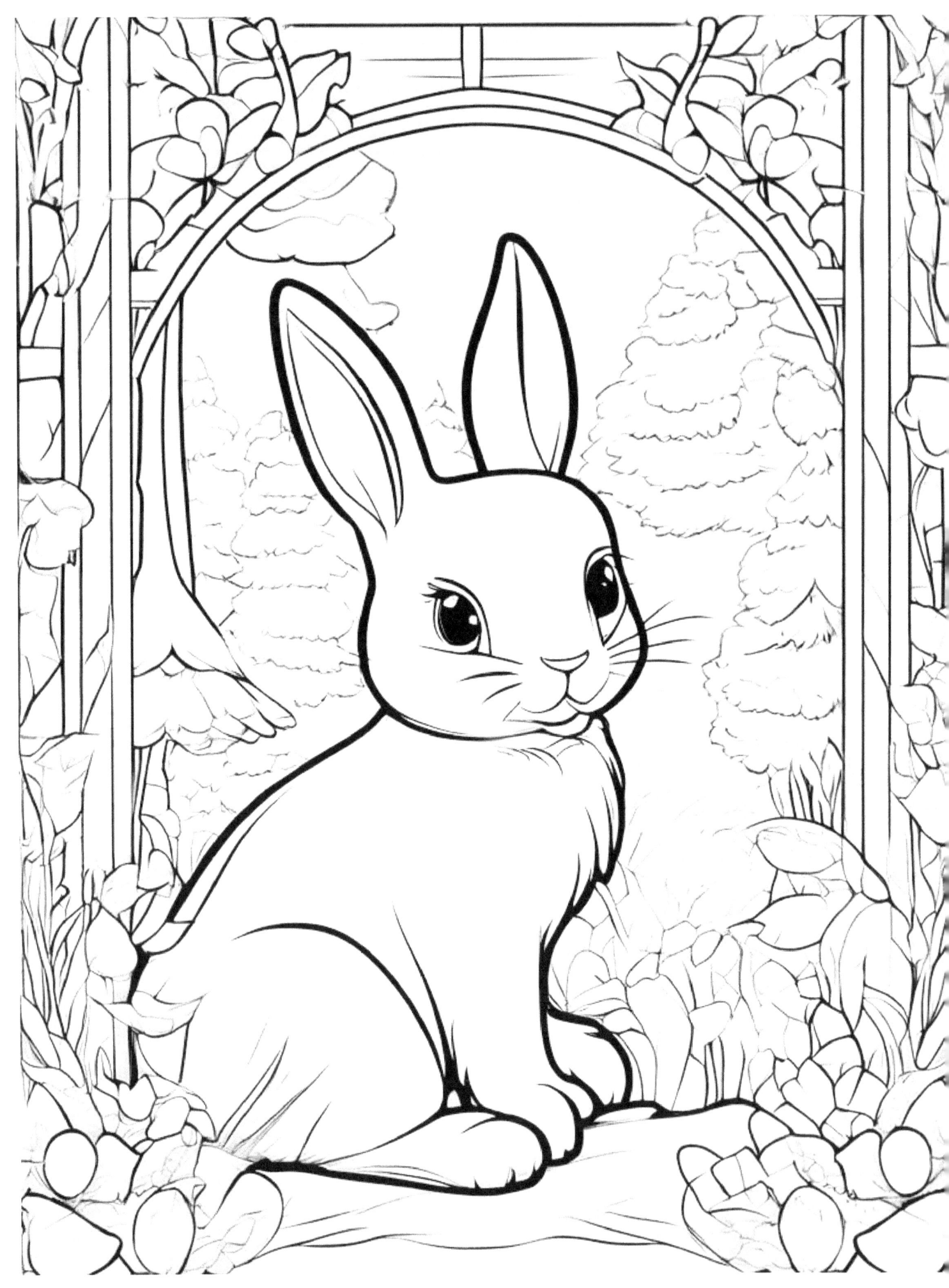

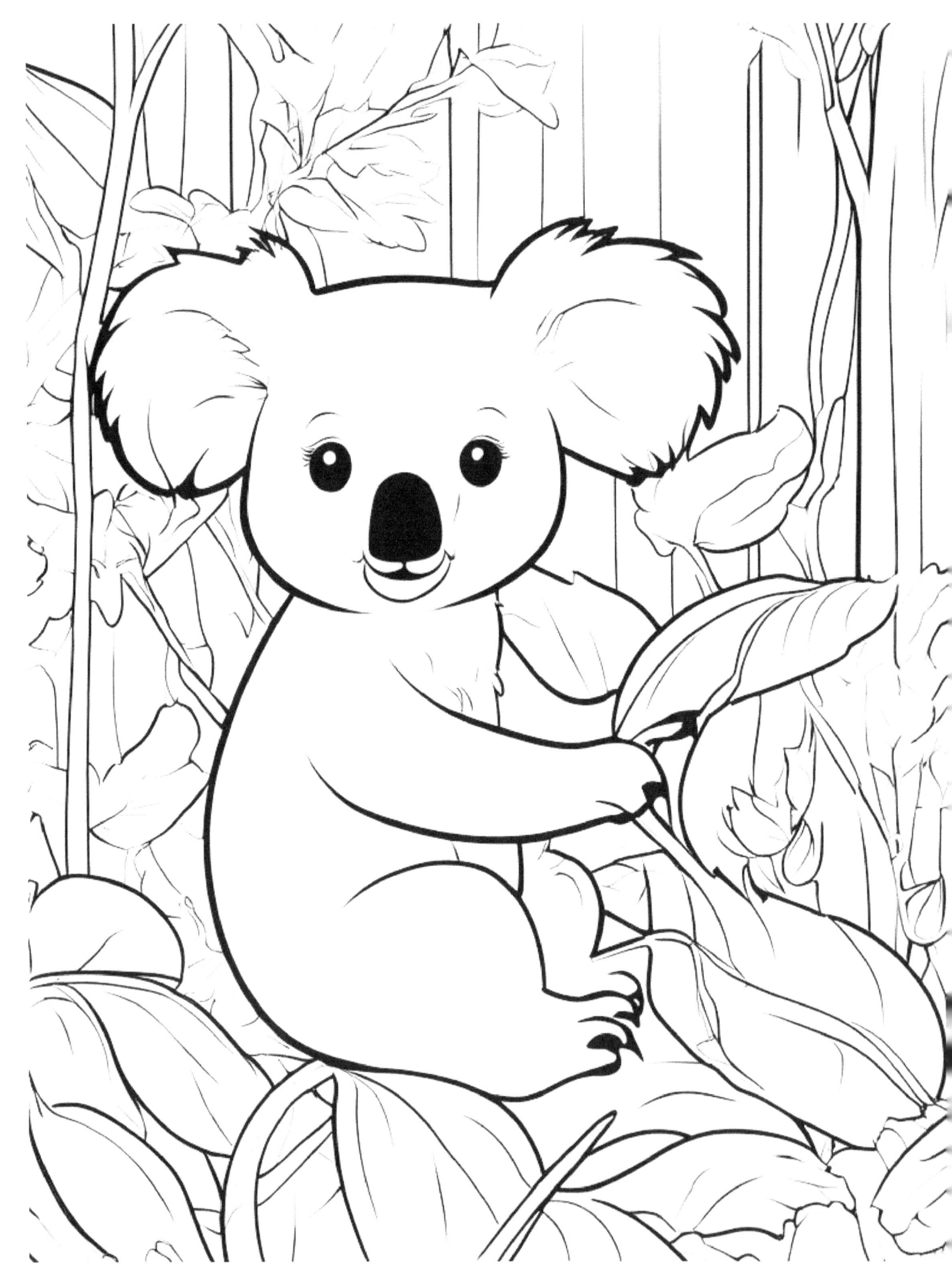

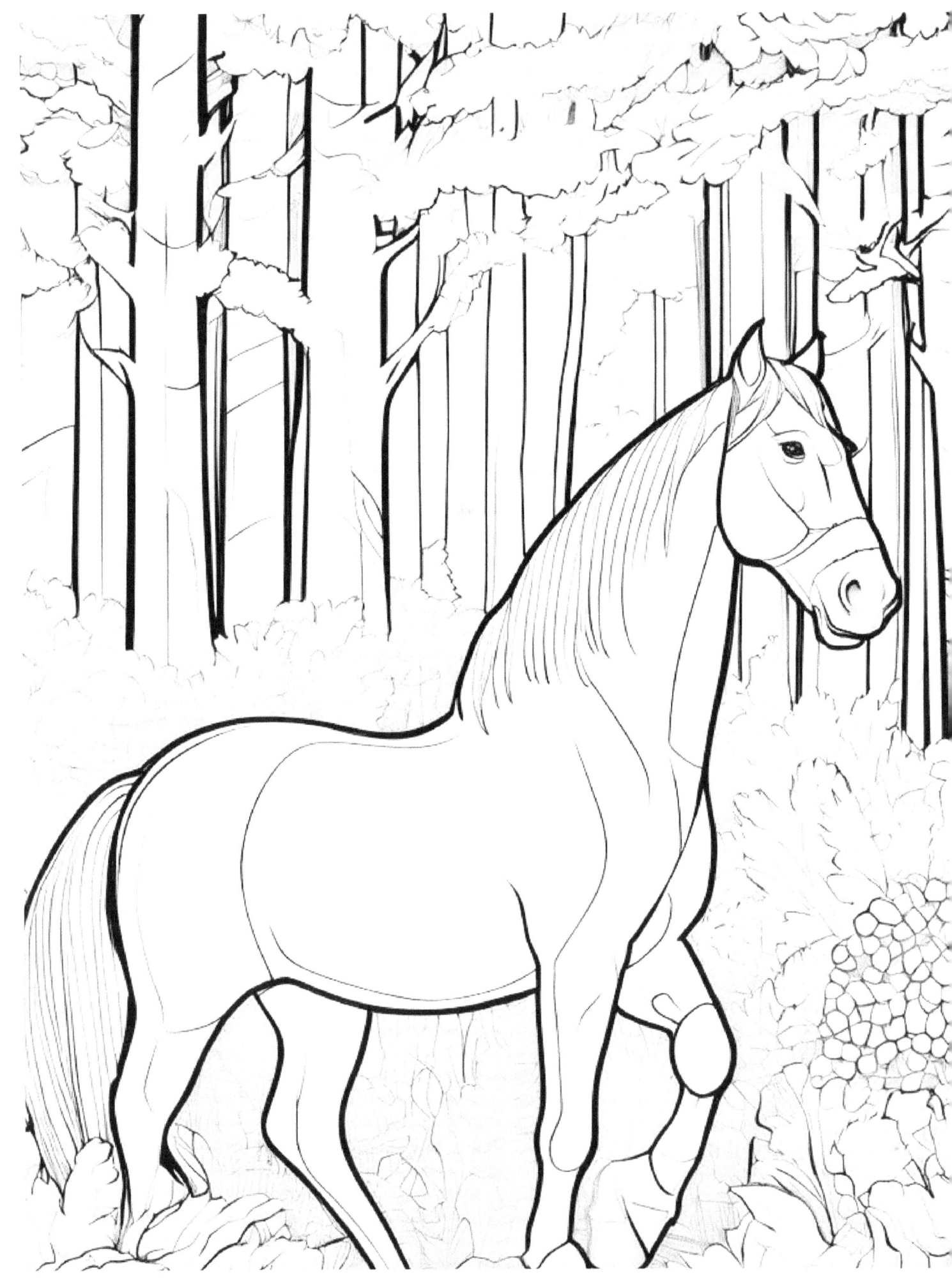

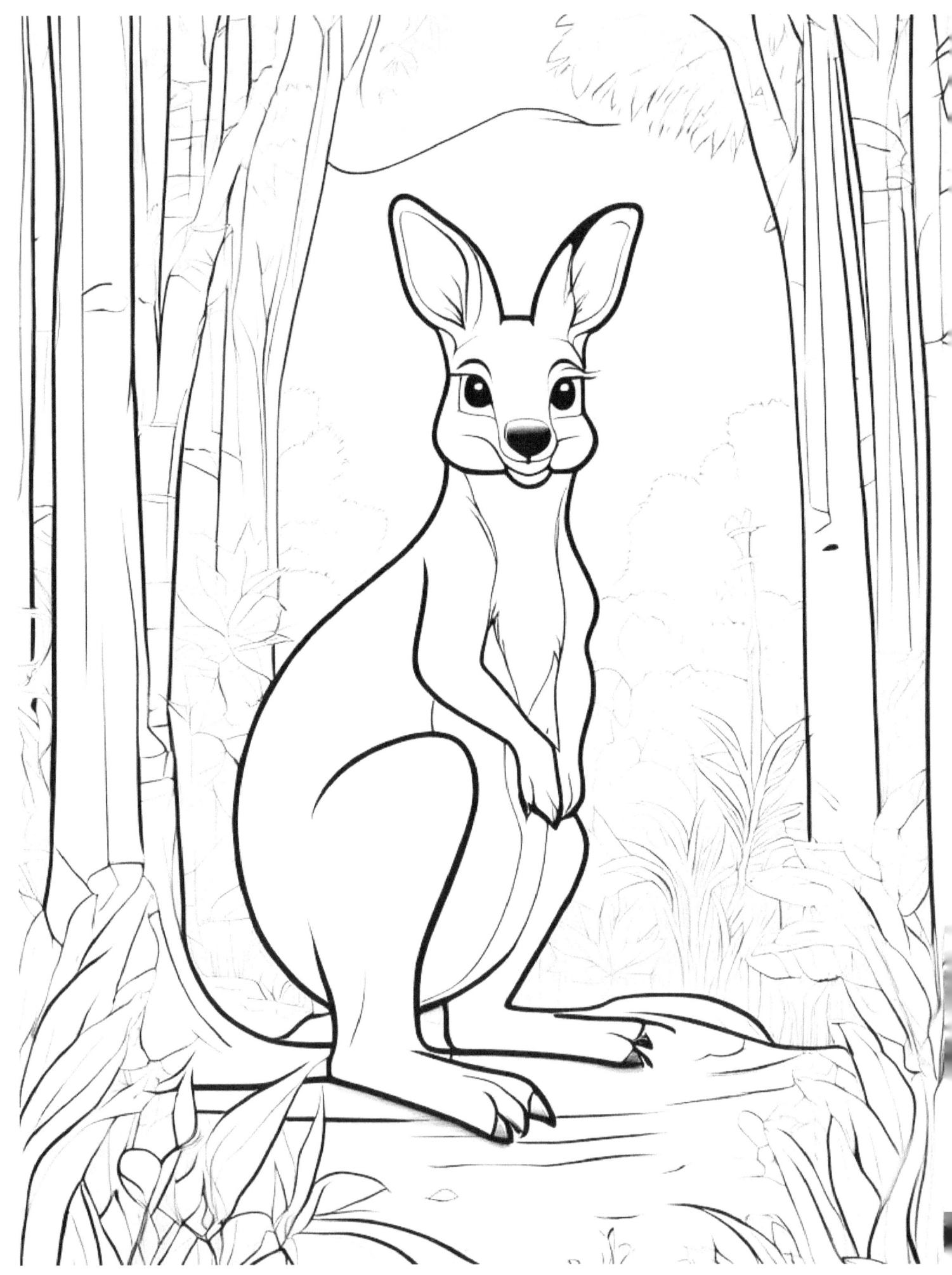

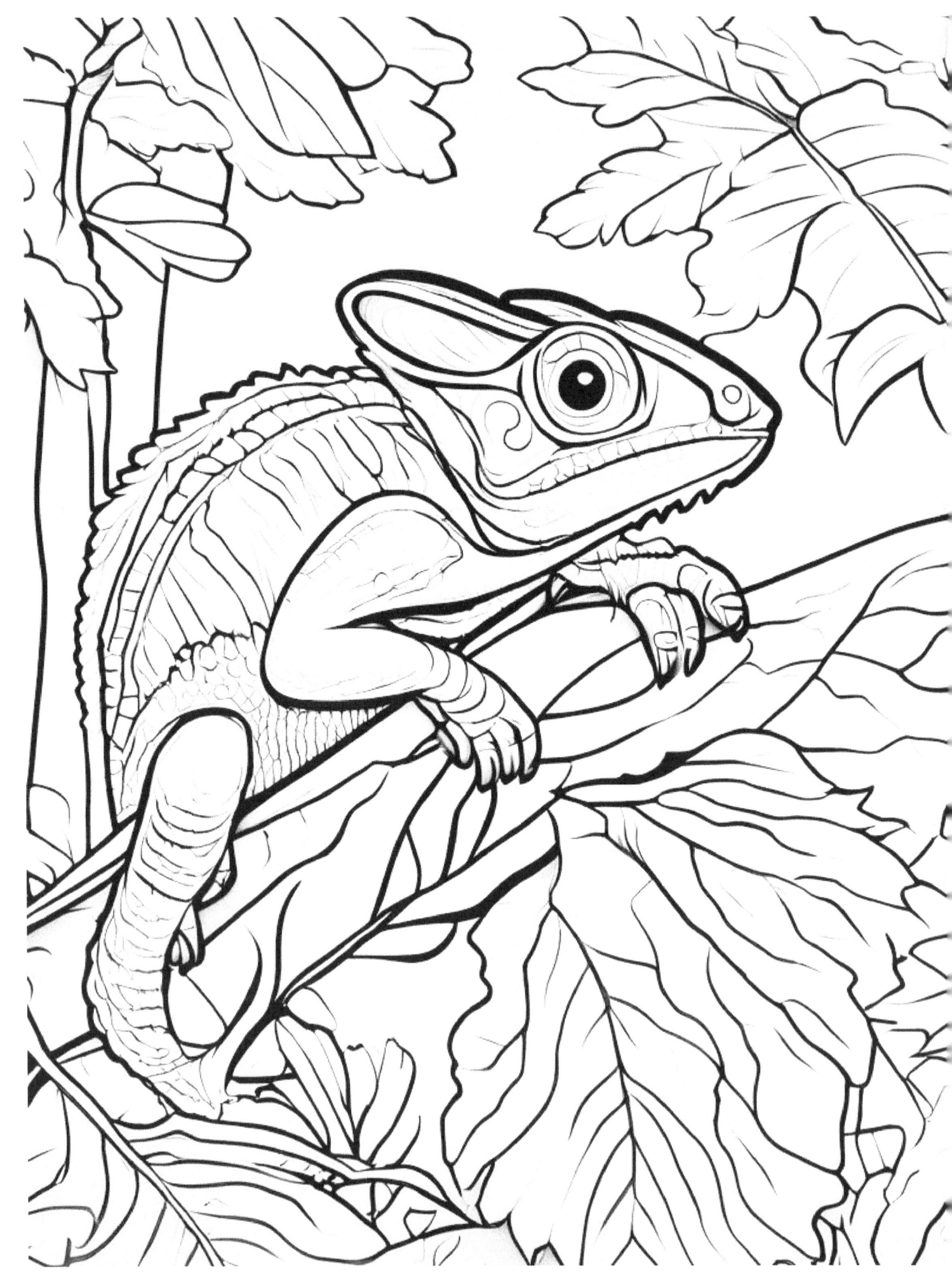

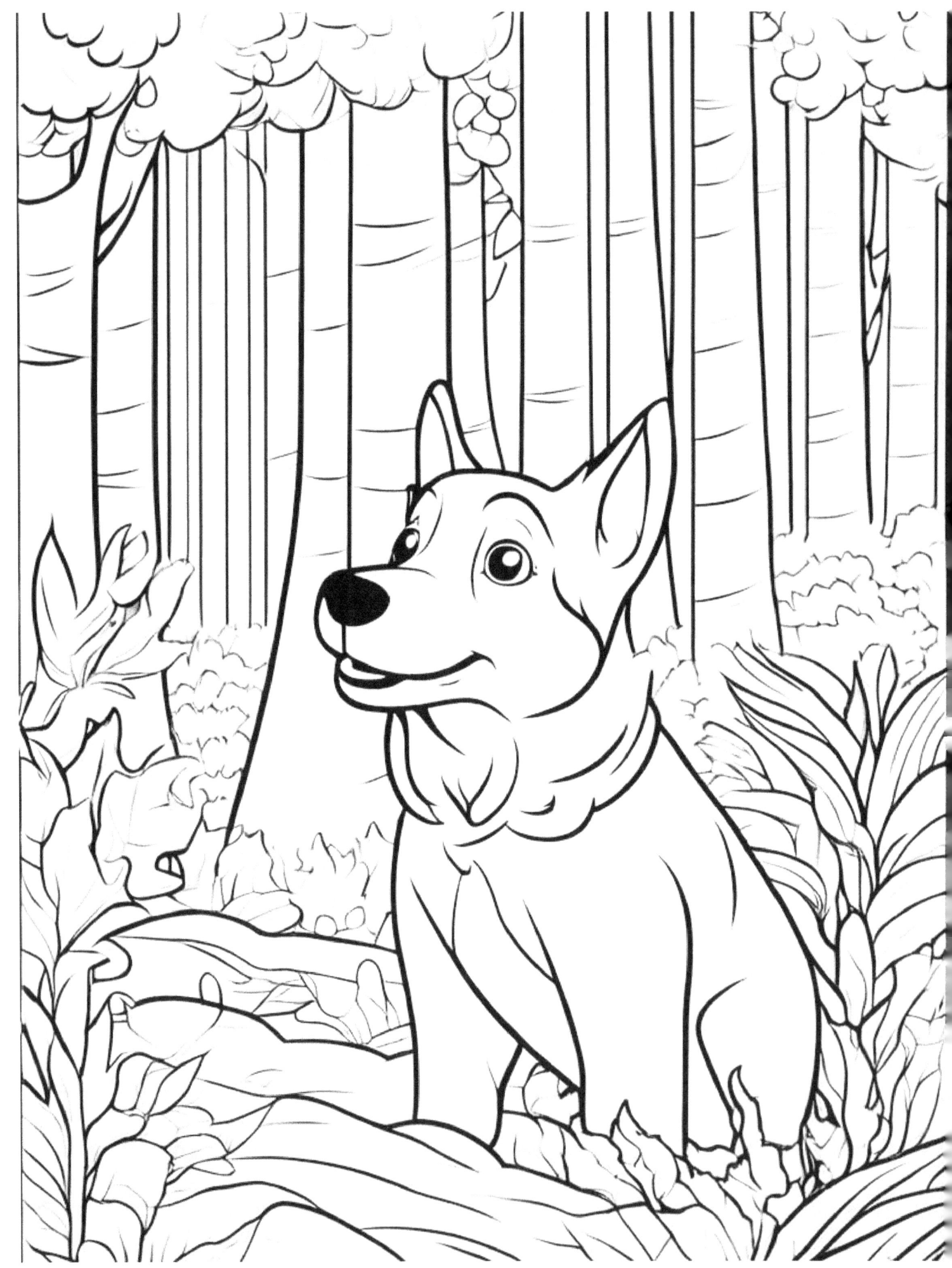

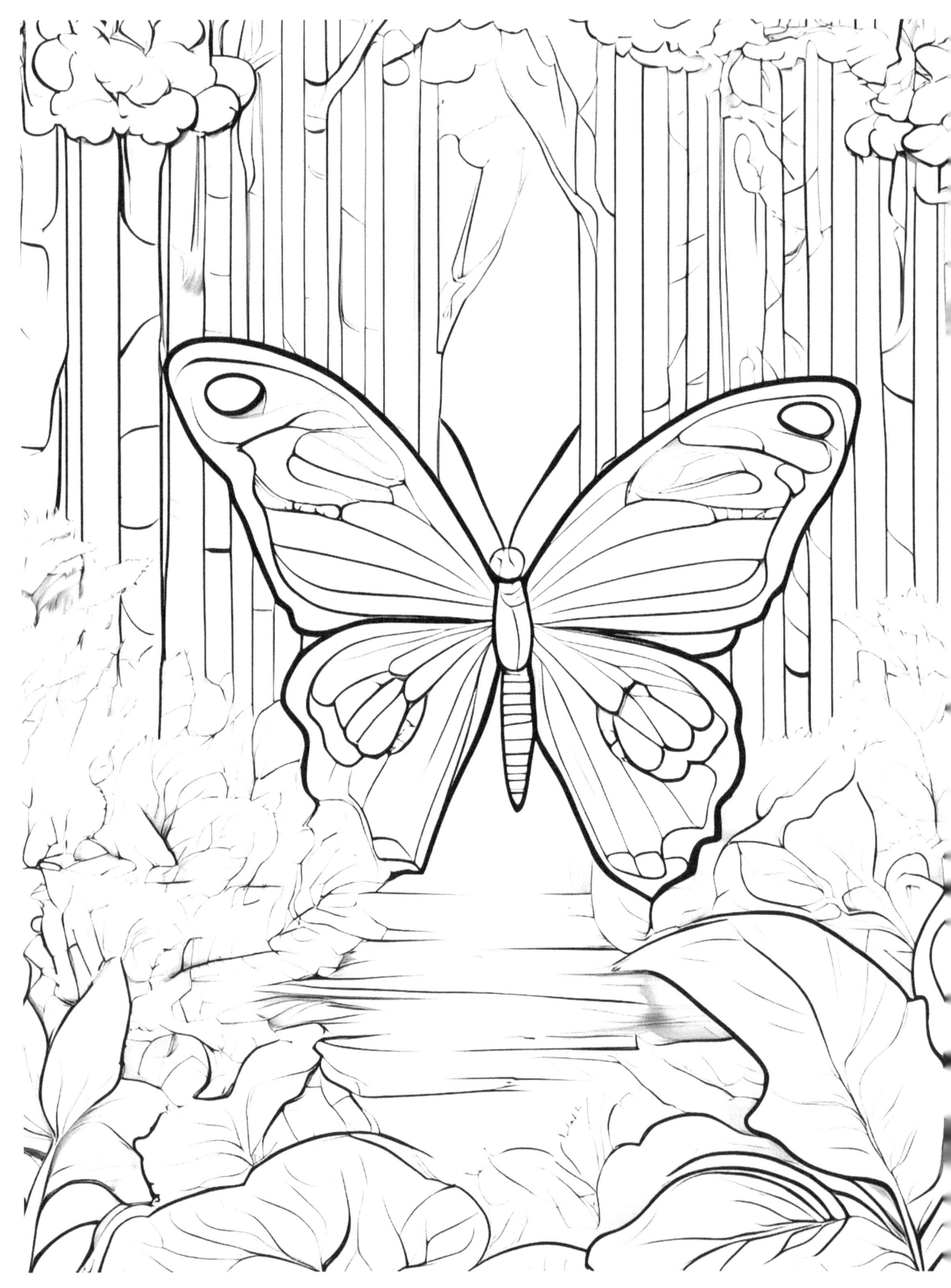

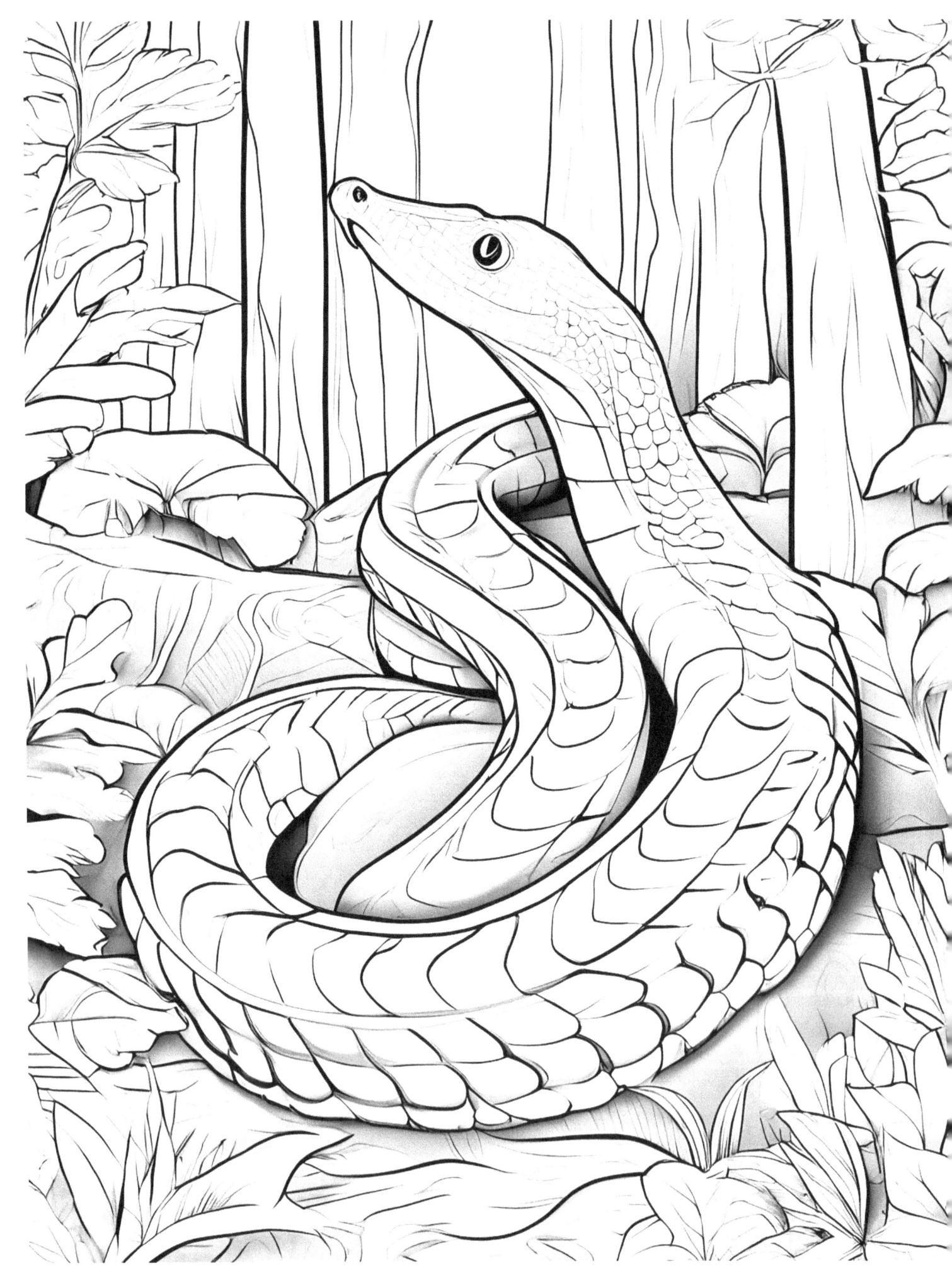

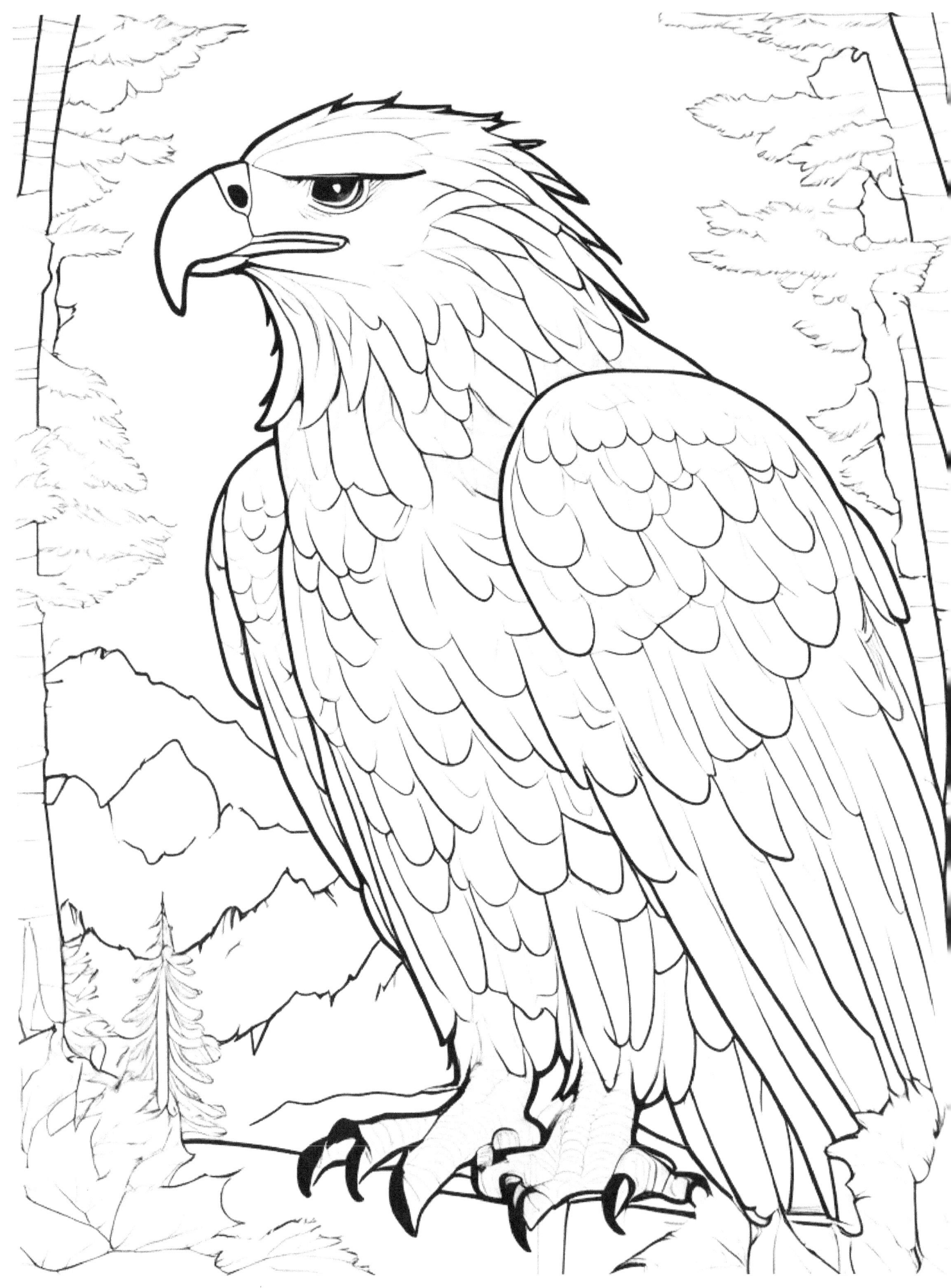

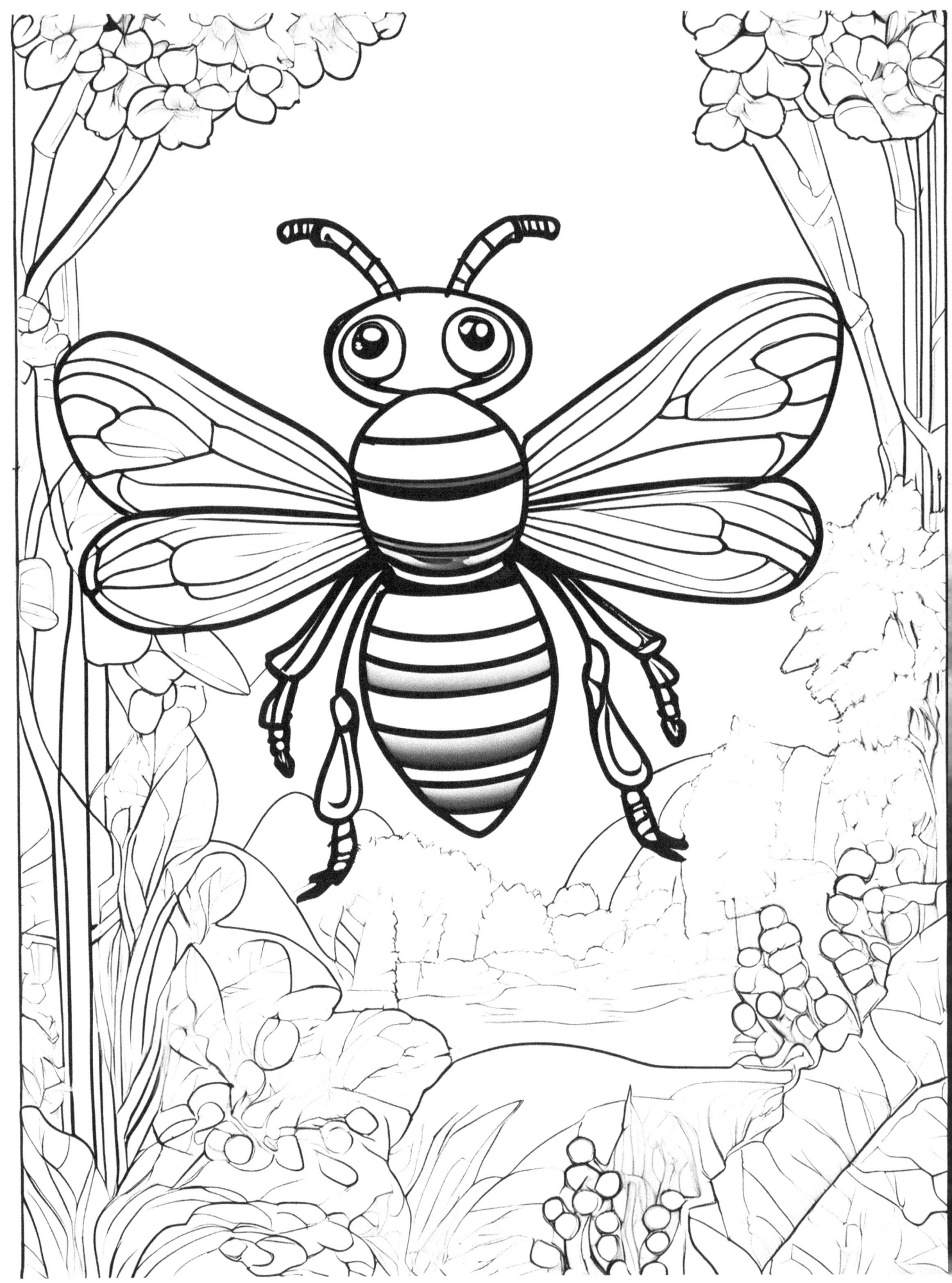

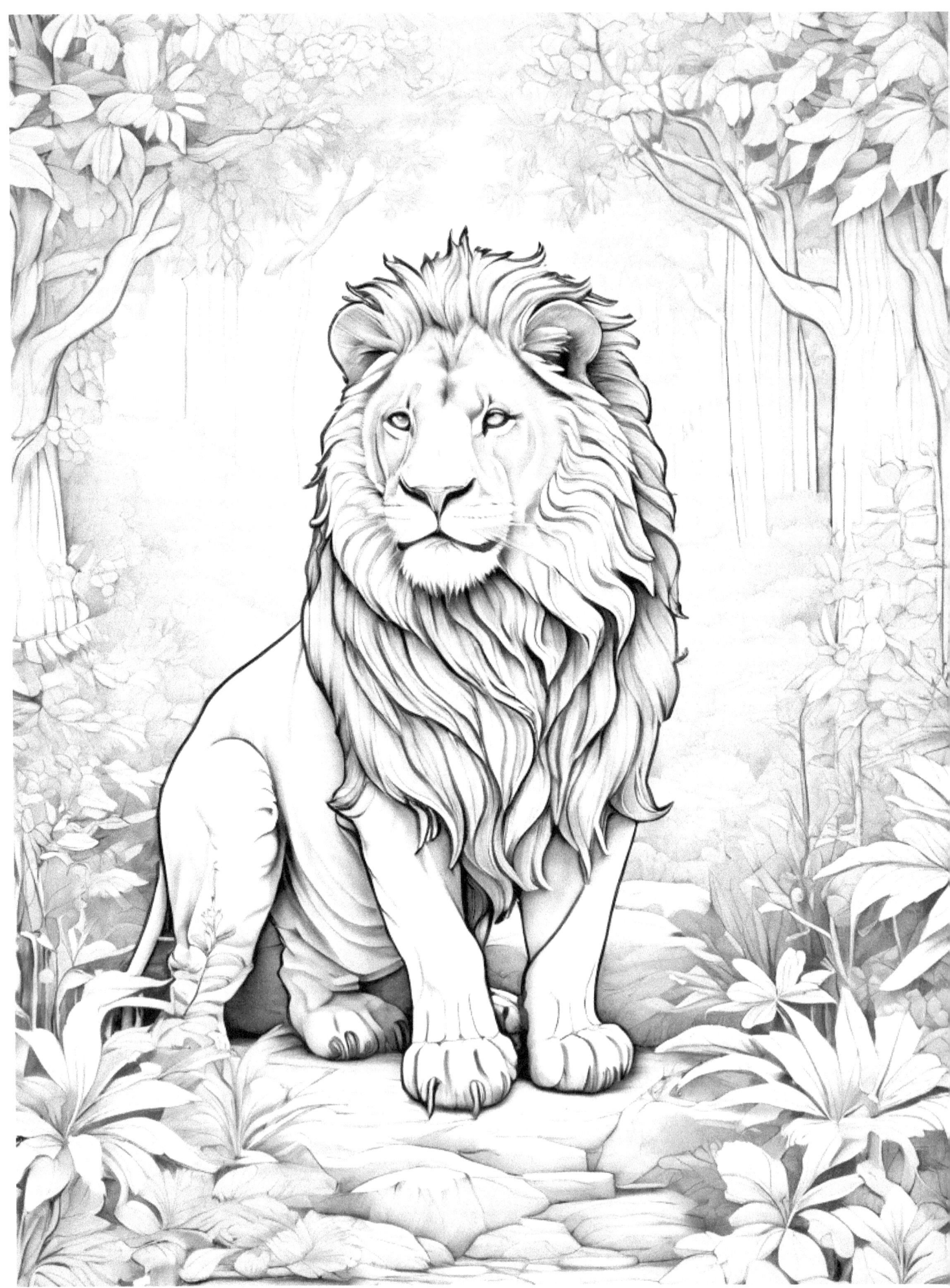